BUILDING ARTS & CRAFTS FURNITURE

25 AUTHENTIC PROJECTS THAT CELEBRATE SIMPLE ELEGANCE & TIMELESS DESIGN

PAUL KEMNER / PEGGY ZDILA

Sterling Publishing Co., Inc. New York

A STERLING/LARK BOOK

Editor: Deborah Morgenthal
Art Director: Dana Irwin
Illustrations: Olivier Rollin
Production: Elaine Thompson, Bobby Gold

Library of Congress Cataloging-in-Publication Data
Kemner, Paul.
    Building arts & crafts furniture : 25 authentic projects that
celebrate simple elegance & timeless designs / Paul Kemner &
Peggy Zdila.
      p.   cm.
    Includes index.
    "A Sterling/Lark book"
    ISBN 0-8069-9418-5
    1. Furniture making--Amateur's manuals.   2. Furniture,
Mission--United States--Amateur's manuals.   3. Arts and crafts
movement--United States--Amateur's manuals.   I. Zdila, Peggy.
II. Title.
TT195.K46   1997
684.1--dc21   96-37210
                                 CIP

10 9 8 7 6 5 4 3 2

A Sterling/Lark Book

Published in 1997 by Sterling Publishing Co., Inc.
387 Park Avenue South, New York, NY 10016

Produced by Altamont Press, Inc.
50 College Street, Asheville, NC 28801

Designs, text, and black and white step-by-step photography
© 1997, Paul Kemner and Peggy Zdila
Color photography © 1997 John Lacy Photography
Additional photography pages 10, 16, 45, 74, and 75, © 1997 Ray Stubblebine

Distributed in Canada by Sterling Publishing
   c/o Canadian Manda Group, One Atlantic Avenue, Suite 105,
   Toronto, Ontario, Canada M6K 3E7

Distributed in Great Britain and Europe by Cassell PLC
   Wellington House, 125 Strand, London WC2R 0BB, England

Distributed in Australia by Capricorn Link (Australia) Pty Ltd.
   P.O. Box 6651, Baulkhaun Hills Business Center,
   NSW Australia 2153

ISBN 0-8069-9418-5

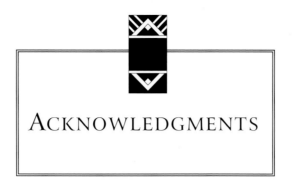

ACKNOWLEDGMENTS

We would like to thank the following people who helped us with our efforts:

Bruce Johnson, for his confidence in us, and for recommending us to Lark Books; Jan Bender, Edward D. and Eve Bunting, Marie Via, Robert Winter, and Ed and Jean Lawrence of the Pebble House Bed and Breakfast for sharing photos of the treasures in their collections; Paul Loguidice, Cyril Keiffer and Brian Burnett, Susan and Alen Roderick, and David Tomsky and the staff at The Grove Park Inn Resort for generously allowing their homes and businesses to be used as photo locations in Toledo, Ohio and Asheville, North Carolina; Dianne Ayres of Arts and Crafts Period Textiles, and Janine Ody of Crystallo for lending beautiful creations which were used in location photography; Tron Turner of The Oakland Museum, Wendy Kaplan and Anita C. Gross of The Wolfsonian, and Catherine Hoover Voorsanger of The Metropolitan Museum of Art who were all particularly helpful with our research. Thanks also to the many staff members at various museums who responded to our inquiries about their collections.

The editor wishes to thank John Lacy for his gorgeous photography of the book projects and for being so patient and flexible; Dana Irwin, whose design for the book beautifully captures the look and spirit of the Arts & Crafts period; Elaine Thompson for tirelessly translating Dana's design into magnificent book pages; Bobby Gold for persisting until the measured drawings were just right; and Olivier Rollin for his elegant illustrations.

■

DEDICATION

This book is dedicated to our fathers and to Gordon and Lorie Wardlaw

and

To other friends, old and new, who made it possible.

CONTENTS

NOTE: Numbers on the right indicate project difficulty, with 1 being easy and 10 being difficult.

It could be claimed that the Arts & Crafts movement has attracted more followers during its current revival than it did during the two decades when its light first burned the brightest. The numerous parallels between the original movement and its current revival—the formation of Arts & Crafts societies, the publication of books and periodicals dedicated to its philosophy, the celebration of annual conventions, the decoration of homes and offices, and a reverence for objects crafted by hand—may lead future historians to declare that the Arts & Crafts movement did not end in 1929 as we of limited vision often recite, but prevailed to the end of the 20th century and beyond.

But while those of us who have embraced the philosophy of simple elegance, clean lines, honesty of materials, and hand craftsmanship espoused by men such as Frank Lloyd Wright, Elbert Hubbard, and Gustav Stickley count ourselves among the faithful, something is missing. We memorize the important dates, we appreciate decorative styles, and we collect the artifacts of an earlier era, but in doing so we too often have denied ourselves the most important element crucial to a complete understanding, appreciation, and enjoyment of the Arts & Crafts movement—the simple joy of creation.

Gustav Stickley did not write for an audience of university scholars, interior decorators, and antique collectors. Instead, he appealed to the craftsman he believed existed within each of his readers. He was understanding of the limitations of space, time, and ability, but he expected that anyone who could appreciate Craftsman furniture, Roycroft metalware, or Grueby pottery would also feel the need and the desire to create for their own homes simple handcrafted objects as an expression of their zeal and appreciation of the philosophy they shared with him.

Most of us were first captivated by the Arts & Crafts style through our Hearts. It is a style not embraced by everyone, but seldom does one smitten by its simple, honest beauty grow unfaithful. It is a movement which also challenges our Heads, enticing us to trace the history of the movement through John Ruskin, William Morris, Gustav Stickley, and Elbert Hubbard. Essays and catalogue introductions are analyzed, memorized, and quoted as if they had sprung from the pen of the Bard of Stratford himself.

But what about the Hand? If, as Elbert Hubbard declared, "The product of the Head, Heart, and Hand is a thing to be loved," then it can only stand to reason that to be completely understood, the Arts & Crafts movement must not be analyzed and adored, but must be experienced with our Hands.

> "THE PRODUCT OF THE HEAD, HEART, AND HAND IS A THING TO BE LOVED."
> *-Elbert Hubbard*

Gustav Stickley also recognized his readers' need for plans and instructions, for guidance and direction of their creative powers. Stymied, in part, by the financial necessity of marketing his own line of furniture, the plans that Stickley published for his readers have proven incomplete. Collectors, scholars, and enthusiasts who have felt the need to create their own Arts & Crafts furniture have been frustrated by the lack of both original models and woodworking techniques unique to the Arts & Crafts style.

Craftsman Paul Kemner and his wife, Peggy Zdila, have generously taken the time to explain for the readers of this book exactly how to build our own Arts & Crafts furniture. Their willingness to share with us the benefit of their years of experience will enable us to appreciate and understand the Arts & Crafts movement completely—with our Head, Heart, and Hands.

Bruce Johnson

Author of The Official Identification and Price Guide to the Arts & Crafts Movement, *Director, Annual Grove Park Inn Arts & Crafts Conference*

I

We wrote this book with the realization that many of those wanting to make one or more of our projects may have little or no prior woodworking experience. We have taken pains to provide more extensive, detailed explanations than what customarily accompanies woodworking projects in books and magazines. We have consciously avoided taking an industrial arts approach to building furniture—precutting and shaping all the parts ahead of assembly. Factories that use this approach build prototypes and sacrifice pieces first to debug their building process, but most home woodworkers want

Instructions for the Large Bookcase begin on page 135.

try skills while restoring and renovating older homes. Sometimes they show us their work. These folks include some of the best proponents of handmade work. We hope they will enjoy this book.

We also meet many antique collectors who, in their pursuit of period furniture, have the same fun we have had with building our pottery collection. Many folks understand style, authentication (well, they know what a factory label looks like), who the reputable dealers are, and provenance. They may even know a few concepts about joinery. But when it comes to differentiating sound and honest construction from less expensive or shoddy methods, they are stuck. One of our goals in creating this book was to help collectors understand how their period pieces were made. We hope we fulfilled this goal and created something of lasting beauty and value for them.

THE ARTS AND CRAFTS MOVEMENT EMPHASIZED THE VALUE OF HANDWORK AND THE PERSONAL INVOLVEMENT OF THE CRAFTSPERSON IN THE CREATION OF A PIECE.

success on their first try. This book was intended for amateurs who will be building in limited quantities. Our hope is to provide them with a satisfactory "tool" for successful project building.

Although we had been considering writing a book about making Arts and Crafts furniture for a year or more, we probably would not have taken the plunge when we did, had Lark Books not come to us first. We meet a lot of weekend woodworkers and a number of folks who develop basic carpen-

The Arts and Crafts revival has created the availability of new furniture and accessories in period style for the home, a circumstance that can be confusing to collectors and home decorators. To understand how furniture is made is to understand what steps in building a piece come at what stage of construction. The Arts and Crafts movement emphasized the value of handwork and the personal involvement of the craftsperson in the creation of a piece. Then and now, handwork is often implied when it is not present, purely as a marketing tool. The next time you see a clever advertisement for manufactured period furniture, ask yourself—what are you really looking at? For example, an ad may include a rough carpentry hand tool, implying that the furniture is handmade. In fact, that tool is being shown in an inappropriate context—with a completed piece of furniture instead of with unfinished lumber. Or, a hand tool may be shown instead of a power tool: nobody doing mass production and marketing can afford to use hand tools. It's a question of economies of scale.

Why the Arts and Crafts Period?

The Arts and Crafts movement appeals to many people today for a variety of reasons. On the most basic and superficial level, its designs are aesthetically pleasing. Good Arts and Crafts design coupled with appropriate and/or traditional materials and good workmanship are a satisfying combination. As the first true contemporary design movement, Arts and Crafts bridges an aesthetic gap between traditional/Victorian interiors and more contemporary ones. This style can be crisp and clean without being cold and sterile, comforting and warm without being cloying.

The movement's ideals still speak to those who understand the meaning of the original Arts and Crafts era to those who lived and worked during that time. The desire to make life less complex, more authentic, more beautiful, more enjoyable, and more meaningful has not left us. Perhaps we crave these things even more now. We may work in paperless offices, and surround ourselves with plastic and other synthetics in clothing, buildings, and vehicles. Real wood, real glass, real pottery, real natural fibers, or even real metal can offer some visual and tactile

relief. Antique or contemporary objects can help to provide this.

Contemporary craftspeople do not just generate products; they instill something of their artistic eye, their care, and their skill in each piece they create. Handcrafted objects embody a special quality never possessed by factory-made goods, and the Arts and Crafts aesthetic adds a style and also a symbolism when used by craftspeople creating objects today.

Our interest in the Arts and Crafts movement began with the purchase of an art pottery bowl in 1986 that started our Arts and Crafts collection. Reading, and eventually attending exhibitions and conferences, deepened our interest, and ultimately culminated in Paul deciding to use his previously acquired skills to create something that was true to the movement. Paul had long known about the movement because of its relationship to the early music revival. (He was an early music performer and undergraduate music major.)

We hope you enjoy the projects in this book. We certainly enjoyed designing and building them. They range from easy to challenging, and reflect the diversity of furniture pieces built during the period.

For some readers, these projects may serve as a catalyst for creating their own designs. To use Arts and Crafts designs as an inspiration for one's own work, one must understand period work. We agree with Gustav Stickley: "Do not think for one moment that you can do good individualistic work until you have demonstrated that you can copy so that the sternest critic must commend what you have done."

Paul Kemner assembling the bookcase.

THE ARTS & CRAFTS MOVEMENT

The Arts and Crafts movement, which flourished in Europe and America from 1870 to 1920, was, in part, a reaction to the cheap imitations of opulent Victorian designs in furniture and home accessories that were becoming available thanks to the growing use of machines. The Arts and Crafts movement promoted and elevated the status of h a n d w o r k , espoused design ideals of beauty, simplicity, and harmony, and encouraged the use of natural materials. The movement is probably best known for the o u t s t a n d i n g workmanship of the handmade objects created during the same period. The relationship of the craftsperson to the object that he or she made was a central element of the movement's philosophy, whether that object was furniture, pottery, metalware, or textiles. Importantly, the design of these crafts aimed to embody British philosopher William Morris's axiom: "Have nothing in your houses that you do not know to be useful, or believe to be beautiful."

These ideals were also applied to the creation of homes; interiors were to be decorated with compatible furniture and accessories, and exteriors were to be landscaped in a simple and natural manner. These goals were championed in America by visionaries such as Gustav Stickley, who manufactured a line of furniture consistent with this style.

Looking beyond the aesthetics of furniture and other objects to the history of the Arts and Crafts movement, it is apparent that it was more than a style, and, in fact, had its own philosophical basis; many called it a social reform movement. Its followers were interested not only in art and craft, but in improving life for everyone by making work more meaningful, homes more relaxing and comfortable, and schools more relevant by teaching trade skills as well as academic ones. Because of these elements, scholars acknowledge that the Arts and Crafts movement was closely related to the turn-of-the-century progressive movement that brought about "good government," garden cities, settlement houses, and other reforms in the United States—which is exactly how Gustav Stickley, one of the Arts and Crafts movement's greatest proponents, described it in his own time.

Art critic John Ruskin and designer William Morris were the leading proponents of the Arts and Crafts movement in Great Britain. Utopian socialists whose political ideas were linked to their opinions about art,

These dining room chairs were made by the Roycrofters for The Grove Park Inn in 1913. In 1919 GPI ordered arms from the Roycrofters and they were attached by Biltmore Industries, Asheville, North Carolina.

"HAVE NOTHING IN YOUR HOUSES
THAT YOU DO NOT KNOW TO BE
USEFUL, OR BELIEVE TO BE
BEAUTIFUL."

–William Morris

*Pewabic Pottery Studio,
Detroit, Michigan*

they lectured and published their opinions about the detrimental effects of the Industrial Revolution on the quality of life, work, and consumer goods. By the end of their lives, both men were regarded as great thinkers and cultural icons. Today, Ruskin is still regarded as an important writer and critic, whereas Morris is most remembered for his contributions to design, although he too deserves credit as a writer and sage.

As the Arts and Crafts movement spread to the United States, much of its political connection was lost. Its goal of democratizing art remained and complemented other progressive aims. Craft communities were organized in America with sometimes only a superficial resemblance to their predecessors in Britain. Under U.S. capitalism, it was difficult for craft communities to remain socialist in practice, and the most utopian of them had a fairly short life span (less than ten years producing crafts).

In America, the most influential tastemaker and proponent of Arts and Crafts philoso-

Arts & Crafts home, Asheville, North Carolina

phy was Gustav Stickley, who not only manufactured furniture, but also published a popular magazine called *The Craftsman*. His magazine aired ideas and news of the progressive movement, and featured stories about Arts and Crafts artisans and their work. It also gave Stickley the opportunity to showcase the style of furniture that he manufactured. Each issue featured his furniture in home settings. In addition, *The Craftsman* regularly sponsored design competitions in which readers were invited to submit scaled drawings of furniture and interior and exterior house appointments and features for competitive cash awards. All entries became the property of the magazine, and it was not unusual to find them published later without attribution to their creators as plans for amateurs to build.

Although many variations of Arts and Crafts architecture evolved and were featured in *The Craftsman*, Stickley was considered to be one of the chief popularizers of the bungalow type home—a one and a half story house with a sloping roof line that sweeps over a porch or veranda. When *The Craftsman* was published, the bungalow style was considered an ideal example of a simple, affordable, attractive and convenient, family-oriented home. When the style was new, the bungalow was humorously described as "a house that looks as if it had been built for less money than it actually cost."

Elbert Hubbard, another popularizer of the Arts and Crafts Movement, established the Roycroft community in East Aurora, New York, where furniture, metalwork, and other crafts were made. During this period when "fine press" publishing was taken seriously as a craft, he also established the Roycroft Press, and published books and two magazines, *The Philistine* and *The Fra*.

Tall clock. Artist: Charles Rohlfs (1853-1936), Buffalo, New York. Oak, copper. The Metropolitan Museum of Art, Gift of Roland Rohlfs, 1985 (1985.261)

Dining room table, sideboard, side chair, and armchair. The Craftsman, *October 1903 Craftsman House, Number IX., Series of 1904*

CLASSIC ARTS AND CRAFTS FURNITURE DESIGNS

In the American style of Arts and Crafts furniture that reached its peak popularity from 1901 to 1915, structure and ornament were united in simple, clean design. Gustav Stickley and his contemporaries in the movement prized designs that expressed honestly, in appropriate materials, the essential qualities of a chair, bed, desk, etc. Structural lines were to be obtrusive, not obscured, and should proclaim the use and purpose of the object and contribute to its decoration. In other words, it was "ornament arising from necessities of construction, and appearing, therefore, spontaneous and natural."

In America, the Arts and Crafts style has popularly been called "mission" style. Stickley never used this label in reference to his own furniture. He preferred the term "Craftsman." Soon after he and others began to make furniture in this style, a clever furniture dealer, who understood the potential popularity of the look, published an ad showing a quaint mission where simple monks handcrafted furniture. The romantic connotation of California missions took hold in the public's mind, and the label "mission" stuck. The label is, however, a poor name for the finer (and more refined) designs from the period, and completely inappropriate for European Arts and Crafts furniture.

The Morris chair, named for William Morris, who designed the first chair of this type, is probably the signature piece of the Arts and Crafts period. Morris chairs were initially of Victorian style when first introduced into the United States in the 1890s. Their features often included round spindles or front posts carved with lion or grif-

Side chair. Artist: Byrdcliffe Colony, 1904. Splat designed by Zulma Steele. Cherry and leather. Milwaukee Art Museum, Layton Art Collection

Morris chair manufactured by the Roycrofters, East Aurora, New York

fin heads. Morris chairs were produced by many manufacturers in the United States and were frequently advertised and pictured in articles on home decoration.

Both Gustav Stickley and his rival manufacturer Elbert Hubbard, as well as others, popularized American Arts and Crafts interpretations of the chair, which were more angular than Morris's original. According to Eileen Boris in her dissertation on the movement (*Art and Labor*, Temple University Press, 1986), "In the public mind, the Morris chair stood for manly comfort." Gus Stickley, however, made "ladies' reclining chairs" as well as large chairs in this style.

". . . IF A ROOM IS PLEASING AND RESTFUL, ONE OF THE HIGHEST AND BEST OF RESULTS HAS BEEN ATTAINED."

—*Gustav Stickley*

Above: Library table. Designer: William Lightfoot Price, Rose Valley (1861-1916). White oak, stained. The Metropolitan Museum of Art, Sansbury Mills Fund, 1991 (1991.145)

China cabinet. Artist: Clarence Albers Zuppann. Collection of Terry and Jan Bender. Photo: Jan Bender

As common as Morris chairs were in home furnishing of this period, they were only a part of the furniture spectrum, which included dining room tables, tabourets, side chairs, bookcases, and many other furniture forms. During an era when reading books and magazines was a popular way for middle-class Americans to relax, the library table was an important part of a properly furnished living room or den. In fact, manufacturers made Arts and Crafts style furniture for virtually every room of the house.

Gustav Stickley manufactured furniture from 1898 to 1916. His is among the best known from the Arts and Crafts period and includes some of the best "design" produced in the period, according to many art museum curators. Over the years of production, however, many labor-intensive details were eliminated from pieces. For example, v-groove plank backs on cabinets were replaced with plywood. Keyed tenons were replaced first with through tenons and then with blind tenons. Perhaps Gus discovered that the average furniture buyer was unwilling to pay for the labor-intensive fine joinery details on his furniture. Or, perhaps rising costs of manufacturing forced him to produce his furniture more cheaply.

But manufactured furniture was not the only kind available in this era that glorified handcraft. Small shops and individual craftsmen made furniture as well. Some of this furniture was designed by architects for specific clients' homes. Today the best known include the Prairie School architects such as Frank Lloyd Wright. Others included Henry Mather Green and Charles Sumner Greene of California.

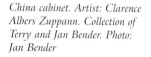

The Work of Individuals and Small Shops

Furniture produced outside of factories during the Arts and Crafts period was made in a number of settings—garages, basements, classrooms, small studios or commercial workshops—by amateur men and women, as well as by professionals. Amateurs worked from published designs and from those they created. Woodworking students created pieces, and their teachers often encouraged them to build original designs or adapt their work from established forms.

Individual craftsmen and woodworkers employed in small shops produced some remarkable examples of case or cabinet pieces, a number of which now reside in American museums or private collections. Many of these pieces were designed as well as executed by the same individual. Cabinet pieces have always been expensive, requiring more materials as well as more time to build than chairs and tables. But cabinet pieces are also canvases for handwork and decorative detail not otherwise common on American Arts and Crafts furniture, and may seem lavish compared to a table or settle. The more highly decorated examples are quite a contrast to the simplicity of factory-made designs attributed to Stickley, whose period designs are still recognized today. The decoration of cabinet pieces reveals a stylistic link with American Colonial furniture makers as well as an aesthetic link between British and American Arts and Crafts furniture. The latter connection was but a part of the spread of Arts and Crafts ideas from Europe to America.

"King Arthur" Chest. Artist: Sydney R. Burleigh. Oak, carved and decorated panels. Museum of Art, Rhode Island School of Design, Bequest of Isaac C. Bates

Secretary and chair. Artist: Harry Napper. Manufacturer: Norman and Stacey, ca. 1901. A good example of English style Arts & Crafts. Mahogany with inlays of light wood in double door upper cabinet and lower drop-front desk, hand-wrought pewter- or zinc-plated metal hardware, door hinges, and drawer pulls. The Wolfsonian Foundation

THE ECONOMICS OF ARTS AND CRAFTS FURNITURE

Today people tend to think that Arts and Crafts antiques are expensive but that the furniture was cheap when it was new. The prices paid for Gus Stickley's furniture during the Arts and Crafts period may seem cheap when compared to 1990s prices for antiques made by his factory or when compared to modern furniture. However, some essential interpretative information is missing. In 1914, the average blue-collar worker made around $11.00 per week (working six days a week). The factory workers who made Gus's furniture could not afford to buy it. It was necessary to be comfortably middle class, a doctor or attorney perhaps, to own it.

Back in 1901, the average annual household income was only $550. Most farms were still worked by human and animal power. Food was expensive, accounting for almost half of the family budget; housing cost nearly one-fifth the family income. After paying for other necessities, such as heat, lighting, and health care, the family had less than $100 to spend on all its other needs and desires. Now compare these costs to the 1904 prices for comparable furniture that Gus actually manufactured and sold: The knockdown settle with a leather seat was priced at $96.50. The slatted reclining chair from Craftsman furniture was $33.00, and the open-arm reclining chair was $26.00. Dining chairs were $7.75 each; a 48-inch bookcase was $37.50; and the 54-inch dining table was $58.00. Gus's furniture was fairly expensive by turn-of-the-century standards. Obviously one needed a considerably above average income to afford it.

Home-built work in The Craftsman, *August 1906*

Fern stand with diamond cutouts. Collection of James and Marie Via. Photo: James M. Via. This piece by an unknown woodworker was made from a plan published in Popular Mechanics. *The "fern stand" in quartersawn white oak is a simple but charming design.*

THE MANUAL TRAINING MOVEMENT

Much of the interest in manual training and industrial arts grew out of the progressive movement and the desire to turn unskilled immigrants and their children into economically independent and respectable members of American society. Gus Stickley was a progressive who espoused both the economic and spiritual advantages of manual training for everyone. In *The Craftsman* he described its positive effect on developing good citizenship and asserted that "Manual training for the child of the city slum is almost the equivalent of life-saving."

Not only were vocational high schools being created, but the manual training movement brought courses in what we now call home economics and industrial arts to many public schools in the U.S. by 1897, according to Sharon Darling in her book, *Chicago Furniture*. Many general high schools introduced shop courses, with woodworking the most popular skill being taught. Some of these schools taught woodworking to girls as well as boys. Manual training came to be regarded as a positive cultural force. Graduates of such training programs were not necessarily prevented from going on to a college or university. The architects Henry Sumner Greene and Charles Mather Greene are prime examples of graduates of manual training programs who went on to higher education and professional careers. In this new climate of appreciation for manual training, publications such as *The Craftsman*, *Popular Mechanics*, *Bungalow Magazine*, and others that featured how-to projects were well received.

Gustav Stickley believed that people love work that they have a natural aptitude for doing and can learn to do this work well. He often wrote about the value of handwork in *The Craftsman*. Here's an example: "The instinct of doing things is a common one, and can be made a source of pleasure, healthy discipline and usefulness, even when the work is taken up as a recreation, and it is this purpose mainly that this series . . . is intended to serve. . . . I should not be true to my own convictions in connection with these cabinet-work lessons, if I did not try to impress upon the reader the value of the moral, mental and physical discipline of manual labor, whether as a daily avocation or a restful and strengthening change for the brain worker in hours of leisure."

Respect for the work of the hand encouraged amateurs to develop their own skills for recreation and personal growth. Crafts that were popular among amateurs during the Arts and Crafts period included all kinds of needlework including appliqué, embroidery, and rug making. Also popular were stenciling, china painting, pottery, pyrography, basketry, woodworking, and metalwork, including vessels and jewelry.

Love of art and the desire for personal growth led individuals to learn a craft, in part, to better understand art. This attitude gave rise to the creation of arts and crafts societies that promoted handwork. In addition, many public museums and academic art programs were created at this time. In fact, a popular culture emerged in America

Table and chairs. Artist: Clarence Albers Zuppann. Collection of Terry and Jan Bender. Photo: Jan Bender

Table made by an amateur woodworker from a Craftsman model. The Craftsman, August 1906

ARTS AND CRAFTS FURNITURE CONSTRUCTION

Honesty and durability in furniture construction were emphasized during the original Arts and Crafts period. When the movement began in England, the emphasis in furnituremaking was on design and handwork. In America, influential furniture "designers" such as Gustav Stickley, along with individual craftsmen, emphasized sturdiness as well as joinery. This established the American Arts and Crafts style in furniture where pieces look "overbuilt." You don't *need* corbels to hold up the top of a bookcase or the arm of a Morris chair. But such ornamental details were symbolic of the concern for sturdiness. The relative abun-

made screws were used sparingly for such tasks as attaching a tabletop, where alternate methods of joinery were not practical. This contrasts to later times when screws became the sole method of joinery. With the advent of machinery came shoddy furniture construction. An example is using butt joints with dowels. Previously, woodworkers had to make their own dowels.

It was as much trouble to make a doweled butt joint as it was to make a mortise and tenon joint. With shoddy construction, little thought was given to wood movement or durability. Today, even high-end manufacturers use their ingenuity to make furniture more cheaply at the expense of durability, but give lip service to quality.

THE ARTS AND CRAFTS HOME

Gustav Stickley believed that Arts and Crafts furniture and architecture were a manifest expression of the structural idea "that reveals, explains, and justifies the reason for

"MANY PEOPLE APPEAR TO IMAGINE THAT THEY CANNOT AFFORD TO HAVE ARTISTIC SURROUNDINGS, WHEREAS THE WONDER IS THAT THEY CAN AFFORD SO MUCH EXPENSIVE UGLINESS." —*Baillie Scott*

Pewabic Pottery Studio, Detroit, Michigan. Photo: Barbara Barefield

dance of timber in the U.S. would have made its liberal use in furniture designs affordable.

As a reaction against shoddy furniture construction, fine Arts and Crafts period furniture was successful. With the advent of the Industrial Revolution, fasteners, such as screws that formerly needed to be hand-made or forged, suddenly became cheap and available in machine-made form for furniture making. In former times, hand-

Contemporary work by Dianne Ayres based on a period design. Arts & Crafts Period Textiles, Oakland, California

the existence of any being, organism, or object." He said that the world had entered "an organic period" which design should reflect. This, of course, brings to mind Frank Lloyd Wright's concept of organic architecture in which the interior of a home, including its furniture, and its exterior, as well as its site, should represent a unified design. Wright, too, in his role in the Prairie School of architecture, may be considered a part of the Arts and Crafts movement.

A lovingly preserved interior in Toledo, Ohio, features textiles collected during the owner's travels. The Arts & Crafts stucco home was built in 1912.

This Arts & Crafts home in Toledo, Ohio, built in 1908, includes an actual period newel post light.

This tile fireplace, a contemporary installation made by Pewabic Pottery of Detroit, Michigan, captures the spirit of the Arts & Crafts movement.

When Arts and Crafts ideals were first interpreted into design, the goal was to make homes more relaxing and comfortable by using interior schemes that met the ideals of simplicity, harmony, and unity of design.

M. H. Baillie Scott, the British architect who was one of the early leaders of the Arts and Crafts movement, believed that furniture should appear "almost to be a piece of the room in which it is placed and in absolute harmony with its surroundings."

This emphasis on harmony and "unity" in interior design explained the popularity of built-in furniture. For example, many period homes have an inglenook, a built-in treatment, used in conjunction with a fireplace to provide intimate and comfortable seating.

Frank Lloyd Wright was especially fond of the way built-ins fit into the composition of

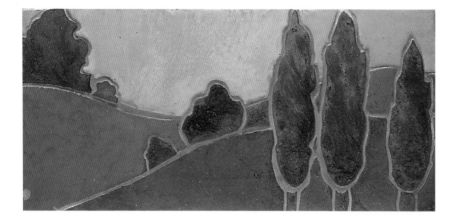

Pewabic Pottery Studio, Detroit, Michigan

Choice in color corresponds to the degree of sensitiveness and education possessed by the eye. The barbarian and the infant seize only the most striking notes in the color-gamut. But as age, training, or civilization advances, the individual appreciates the semi-tones, the quarter-tones, perhaps even the finer divisions of the chromatic scale

Page reproduced from The Craftsman

a house interior. He liked the focal point of an inglenook and always included a fireplace in his home designs. Like other period architects, he felt that the hearth was a natural gathering place for the family. Built-ins prevent some problems in arranging furniture. According to Baillie Scott, one of the main faults in furniture placement was overcrowding. He recommended that homeowners avoid crowding rooms with possessions, take out everything nonessential, and strive to have "a few choice things rather than many inferior ones."

Armed with some knowledge of the Arts and Crafts aesthetic, today's home decorator can recreate the beauty and charm of the "Craftsman" home. An idyllic vision of "The Modern House Beautiful" was described by a writer in *The Craftsman* in this way: "The living room is imbued with a spirit of companionship and hospitality. There are deep inglenooks, bright log fires, musical instruments, tea-tables, and windows full of soft sunshine and bright flowers. . . . the nurseries are full of the spirit of childlife and recollections from fairyland. . . . The study is cozy, with low bookcases, writing desks, and reading lamps."

Advice on home decoration in *The Craftsman* always emphasized the importance of an effective and sensitive treatment of the woodwork in a room. Use of a color appropriate to the wood being used set the stage for the rest of that room's decoration. Homebuilders were encouraged to use indigenous materials to make the house blend with the landscape. For use in interior woodwork, tulipwood was more available in certain areas, oak in others, and gum or chestnut elsewhere. Likewise, for exteriors and for interior features such as fireplaces, certain regions had a more ready supply of stone. The effect of using local building materials often achieved a vernacular architectural style.

Again writing in *The Craftsman*, Gustav Stickley asserted: "If the woodwork of your house is finished so that the natural beauty of the wood is enhanced; if the same thing were done in the furniture; and you then see that the color scheme of woodwork, furniture and hangings harmonize, you cannot fail to secure in each room a charm and beauty that is a great step accomplished towards the simplicity and restfulness that is so desirable to gain. For let it never be forgotten that if a room is pleasing and restful, one of the highest and best of results has been attained."

An atmosphere of comfort and repose was the goal of decorative treatments for interiors. These included friezes or deep borders on walls near the ceiling, which were often stenciled; grass cloth or canvas as a wall covering; decorative tiles, especially for fire-

Open Frame Flat-Arm Morris Chair (page 105), Straight-Sided Footstool, (page 91), and Large Round Tabouret (page 56)

places (matte glazed tiles were particularly favored); wainscoting, paneled walls, and beamed ceilings. Transparent, and frequently textured, colored glass panels for windows, cabinet inserts, doors, etc., were used in green and amber tones. Stained glass was still used, but art-glass windows were usually more restrained in their use of color than in Victorian times. Panels with beveled glass or large areas of clear glass accented with touches of color were also popular.

Decorative accents recommended as hardware for door knobs and pulls on built-in cabinets and drawers included brass, wrought iron, copper, and wood. Accessories suggested for decorating rooms included potted plants, pottery, basketry, and hand-hammered metalwork. Handmade rugs were preferred. Compatible rugs included American Indian, East Indian Drugget, Oriental, Donegal types in Morris or Voysey patterns, and hooked or braided. Furniture upholstery was often leather or canvas.

Various shades of earth tones were usually suggested for downstairs rooms. Home decorators aimed for a cordial, welcoming atmosphere for the "public" rooms. Preferred color combinations included gray-green for walls with cream for the ceiling, and golden brown for walls with pale green for the ceiling.

Other recommended colors included shades of yellow, moss or olive green; beige, browns, rusts or russets; and touches of orange, dull or dark red, or deep blue. Naturally derived colors inspired by stone, brick, and wood were popular for interiors, just as use of these elements in building was encouraged for the structure of the home itself.

A delicate look was recommended for bedrooms, where the woodwork was frequently painted or a lighter color wood or stain was used. Colors suggested for walls included soft gray-blue with white; light sage green and ivory; or pale yellow and seal brown with touches of orange. Linen bedspreads, often embroidered or appliquéd, were considered desirable. Home decorators were cautioned to be conscious of a room's location on the sunny or shady side of the house before choosing colors.

Emulating the beauty of the outdoors, *The Craftsman* decorating scheme aimed for an effect in which the look of the interior elements would change, and its charm "increase as changing seasons and varying days reveal accidents of light and shade, of color and tone."

"The beauty of simplicity and restraint" in home furnishing is a recurring theme in period writing about the Arts and Crafts style. A practical virtue of the fewer-furnishings philosophy is its positive effect on housecleaning. In fact, the turn of the century was a period when people were especially concerned about cleanliness, sanitary conditions, light and air, and a healthful lifestyle. Outdoor living was desirable as were sleeping porches and porches of all kinds, gardening, and outdoor structures such as pergolas. Then as now, people of the Arts and Crafts era appreciated features in home design that allowed them to "bring the outdoors in" and thereby enjoy their homes and lives more fully.

NATURE AND THE HOME

"**I**n the arrangement of a home, Nature, culture, and common sense should supply the guiding principles. . . .Nature will offer unfailing suggestions as to the color most wholesome and agreeable to the eye; culture will discard vulgarity and display; common sense will decide between the useful and the useless, always rejecting that which, too fine for daily use, will remain an alien element in the home; rigidly examining all ornament as if it were a suitor for entrance to the family circle; questioning every object eligible for admission, lest, after acquiring it, the owner should raise his standard of taste and the thing acquired become hateful to him."

—*Gustav Stickley*

Etching. Artist: Harold L. Doolittle. Entitled "Giant Redwoods," measuring 10" x 12". Collection of Edward D. and Eve Bunting. Themes of nature were important philosophically, and were popular for decorating during the Arts and Crafts Movement. Doolittle was an artist and craftsman in many media. Photo: Sloan Bunting

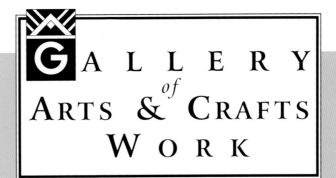

GALLERY
of
ARTS & CRAFTS
WORK

Drop front desk, chair, and wastebasket. Artist: Clarence Albers Zuppann. Desk is marked "Sept. 1, 1909, Turner Street School." Collection of Terry and Jan Bender. Photo: Jan Bender

Fir chair with heart cutout. This chair may have been the work of a Throop Polytechnic student. Photo: Robert Winter

Shakespeare chest. Designer & decorator: Sydney R. Burleigh. Cabinetmakers: Potter & Co., ca. 1900. Ebonized cherry with painted panels. Museum of Art, Rhode Island School of Design, Gift of Ellen D. Sharpe. Photo: Del Bogart

English or English-inspired, this leaded glass book-case of unknown origin, features a motto character-istic of the period. Collection of The Grove Park Inn

Nicknamed the "Martian Clock" for its unusual shape and top, this clock features an oak case with metal and glass detailing. It was handmade by an unknown crafts-man. Collection of Dr. Robert Winter (alias "Bungalow Bob"). Photo: Robert Winter

Lamp. Artist: Gerald "Hop" Harlan Eggers. Collection of Jean and Ed Lawrence. Photo: Paul Kemner

American library table of unknown origin. Its most distinctive features are its splayed legs and its quartersawn oak ray-flake patterns. Collection of The Grove Park Inn

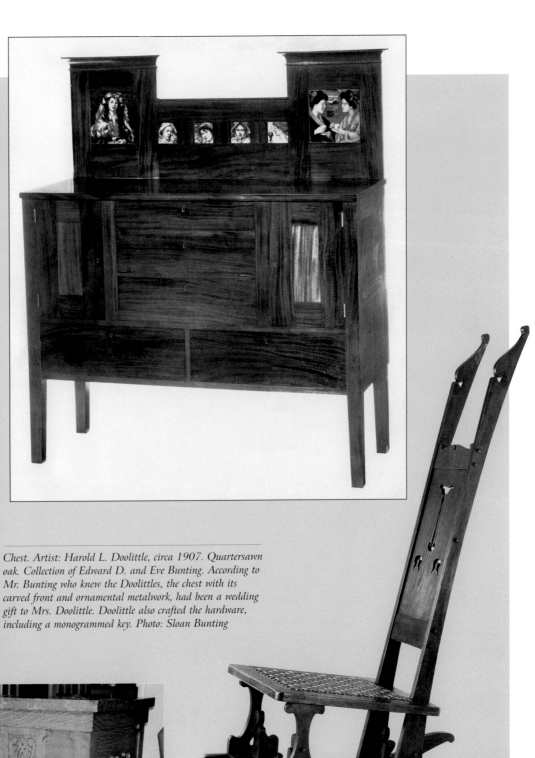

Sideboard. Artist: Sydney R. Burleigh, Fleur-de-Lys Studio, Providence, Rhode Island, (1895-1910). Mahogany, oil painting. Sideboard with three drawers flanked by a cupboard door over two half drawers. In the background are six oil paintings, each depicting a woman in a foreign land in her native dress, either drinking or dispensing the drink of her country. Henry Ford Museum & Greenfield Village

Chest. Artist: Harold L. Doolittle, circa 1907. Quartersawn oak. Collection of Edward D. and Eve Bunting. According to Mr. Bunting who knew the Doolittles, the chest with its carved front and ornamental metalwork, had been a wedding gift to Mrs. Doolittle. Doolittle also crafted the hardware, including a monogrammed key. Photo: Sloan Bunting

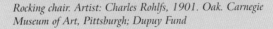

Rocking chair. Artist: Charles Rohlfs, 1901. Oak. Carnegie Museum of Art, Pittsburgh; Dupuy Fund

Arts & Crafts homes: Toledo, Ohio, and Asheville, North Carolina

Oak chest. Designer: Probably Ralph Radcliffe Whitehead (1854-1929). Panels designed by Edna M. Walker. Maker: Byrdcliffe Colony, Woodstock, New York. Oak, tulip poplar, brass. The Metropolitan Museum of Art, Purchase, Friends of the American Wing Fund and Mr. and Mrs. Mark Willcox, Jr. Gift, 1991 (1991.311.1)

ART *and* PHILOSOPHY *of* WOOD SELECTION

In this section I will discuss the challenges of purchasing wood and selecting boards to use in particular projects. In general, what is required is aesthetic judgment, although common sense will also guide you.

EMPHASIS ON LOCAL MATERIALS

In America during the Arts and Crafts period, the use of native hardwoods in architecture and furniture was highly valued. The use of local materials was emphasized (a carryover from the British Arts and Crafts movement). Because it was acceptable to use local materials during this period, a true vernacular approach to using lumber and other building materials developed. This idea was articulated by William Morris,

whose writings were highly respected. According to Morris, "Good decoration, involving rather the luxury of taste than the luxury of costliness, will be found to be much less expensive than is generally supposed."

Gustav Stickley, who was a follower of Morris, said that the goal was to "substitute the luxury of taste for the luxury of costliness; to teach that beauty does not imply elaboration or ornament; to employ only those forms and materials which make for simplicity, individuality and dignity of effect."

Although many different hardwoods and softwoods were used for decorative woodwork in Arts and Crafts

Detail of Clarence Albers Zuppann's bookshelf. Collection of Terry and Jan Bender. Photo: Jan Bender. Photo of bookshelf appears on page 83.

ADAPTING TRADITIONAL STICKLEY DESIGNS TO TODAY'S LUMBER

The surviving Gustav Stickley pieces exhibit more variation than one would expect from factory-made work today. Factories at that time made furniture in batches, patterns and templates wore out and were replaced, and the dimensions varied slightly from batch to batch. Also, in general, earlier examples of the same design use thicker wood. A table may have started out with a full 1⅜"-thick top, and 12 years later the same design was made with a 1"-thick top.

I have tried to present designs that can be built from contemporary commerically cut lumber—mostly 5/4 rough thickness. In my opinion, religious adherence to the drawings and dimensioning to 1/64th of an inch is not as important as the general proportions and original construction details. Proportion, wood selection, consistency in the way you relieve sharp edges, joinery, and finish quality are hallmarks of a successful Arts and Crafts furniture piece.

---

period homes, furniture, at least of the manufactured variety, was a different matter. The factory furniture that was made during this period set the style, and the wood most emphasized was quartersawn white oak, usually in medium to dark finishes, and often in massive-looking designs. This posed quite a visual contrast to earlier mass produced "golden oak" furniture such as pressed-back chairs and other furniture "hand carved" by machines.

QUARTERSAWN VERSUS STRAIGHT-SAWN WOOD

There are several ways to cut a tree-trunk into a stack of flat boards. The most common today is called *straight- or slab-sawn* (figure 1).

Quartersawing (figure 2) saws or splits the log into quarters, which are then sawn into boards. The boards are narrower, but are less prone to warping, and are more stable. In addition to giving a finer appearance, quartersawing also reveals a handsome "ray flake" figure in some species of wood. These woods have cellular structures called *medulary rays* that radiate from the center of the tree, and where they intersect with the face of the board, they produce an iridescent pattern.

Wood swells and shrinks with changes in humidity. A slabsawn board will swell and shrink *twice as much in width* as a quartersawn board. This means that furniture made from quartersawn wood will be more stable, and less likely to suffer from splits, cracks, and broken joints.

The easiest way to identify quartersawn wood is to look for the tree rings at the end of a board. The rings will run vertically, and you will see the rings as parallel lines on the face of the board. In a slabsawn board, the

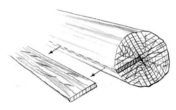

figure 1
Straight-sawn lumber

figure 2
Quartersawn lumber

rings will run horizontally, and make a characteristic arch pattern on the face. In *rift-sawn* boards, the rings are at approximately 45 degrees.

Sawmills like to slabsaw because it yields several wide boards and minimizes the number of times the log must be turned during the sawing process. Conversely, most sawyers regard quartersawing as "wasteful" because it produces fewer wide boards. Ironically, they may be sawing the same species for pallet lumber.

DERIVING QUARTERSAWN LUMBER FROM THROUGH AND THROUGH SAWING

Large commercial sawmills can cut logs in such a way that no quartersawn lumber is produced. Some small sawmills do a type of sawing called *through and through*. This process involves making horizontal cuts through a log from top to bottom. Some quartersawn lumber can be obtained from the same operation that produces slab-sawn boards, due to the position of particular boards in the cutting. The center boards are essentially quartersawn, but need to be cut into two pieces with the center (or pith) removed. A few boards with quartersawn grain are thus obtained from each tree and sorted out and sold as quartersawn lumber. If these boards are dried properly they can be useful.

Keep in mind that only a few boards in each bin or stack are from the same tree. These different trees may have grown in different soil or even be of different species classified as "white oak." (*Quercus alba* v. chestnut oak v. swamp oak, etc.) The bottom line is that with mixed boards from different sources, the boards will take your finish differently. This goes double for ammonia fuming. With small projects where you can get all of your wood from one board, it won't matter. For larger pieces you will definitely see a difference. Of course, you can use this effect intentionally to achieve interesting results.

Quartersawn White Oak

Traditionally, quartersawn white oak was a favorite wood for making whiskey barrels and also for shipbuilding, as its tight pore structure gives water resistance, and also adds to its strength. Gustav Stickley agreed that quartersawing wood increases its strength and durability. (For example, a quartersawn oak floor is less likely to warp or splinter than a slab-sawn floor.)

Quartersawn white oak was the wood of choice for furnituremaking during the Arts and Crafts period. In its most noble incarnations as finely crafted furniture, it was treated by ammonia fuming to enhance the look of its finish. The wood was admired chiefly for its striking ray flake figure and for its susceptibility to ammonia fuming, a process that naturally darkens some woods. It was seen as a beautiful wood when appropriately handled.

For the woodworker today, however, this beauty comes with a price. The long drying time required for this wood (the longest of any domestic hardwood, to my knowledge) means that not many commercial sawyers want to handle it. Many who do process it do so primarily for overseas shipment for flooring and building construction. The drying time required to prepare wood for overseas shipment to more humid climates is less than that required for domestic furniture lumber.

Today, the best commercially available hardwood for furniture making is kiln dried. (This is important because today's furniture resides in centrally heated homes. When homes were not centrally heated, the percent of dryness of furniture wood was not as critical, because it was not exposed to dramatically different humidity conditions.) In the lumber trade, boards are cut to size before being kiln dried, so they go into the kiln looking basically the same as when they come out of the kiln.

Due to quartersawn white oak's long drying time, lumber available for sale may be improperly dried. Quartersawn white oak, like any other wood, must be dried to a seven percent moisture content for use in furnituremaking. Although white oak takes longer to dry than most native hardwoods, quartersawn white oak takes longer still. Some commercial drying kilns that do not specialize in white oak will run the boards through the kiln with a load of red oak at the same speed as the red oak, instead of giving the white oak its necessary drying time. This is a recipe for drying defects. If improperly dried, white oak is prone to internal checking, cracking, and splitting. It is heartbreaking to spend hours planing and cutting boards only to discover, when you cut a board to final size or cut a tenon, a hidden defect that makes the wood damaged beyond use.

When quartersawn white oak is dried too fast, a drying defect called *honeycombing* occurs. Honeycombing is a type of internal checking. The outside of the board can appear just fine. It is very common for drying defects to be invisible on the outside and appear only when boards are cut to final size by the woodworker.

The quartersawn grain of this bookcase is accented by hand-hammered copper pulls by Chris Efker's Craftsman Hardware.

It is difficult nowadays to find wide boards and thicker stock in quartersawn white oak lumber. Much of the wood is sawn to size for flooring. (There is a lot of ¾" lumber out there.) The best advice I can give is to know your supplier. I generally like the ones who cut and dry the wood themselves. I like to know where my wood comes from, who dried it, and exactly how it was cut. You might want to know your lumber dealer's return policy before you buy. Once you make your purchase, it's a good idea to make a set of bookends or another small project before planing or cutting the other boards.

Because of the difficulty in obtaining good quartersawn white oak lumber, folks who want to build Arts and Crafts style furniture may want to consider using another hardwood.

OTHER HARDWOODS

Other hardwoods worthy of consideration for building Arts and Crafts style furniture include mahogany, ash, elm, cherry, chestnut, red oak, and straight- or slab-sawn white and red oak.

White Oak ▪ Although straight- or slab-sawn white oak is generally more readily available than quartersawn white oak, it is still prone to drying defects due to improper drying. Be careful.

Ash ▪ Ash is usually less expensive than white oak and has a similar coarse grain structure. In fact, antique pieces from the period identified as oak are sometimes actually made of ash. At least one Arts and Crafts period manufacturer produced a lot of ash furniture. Ash does not have a noticeable flake figure when quartersawn. But if you like a light-colored finish, ash may be an especially good choice because,

Detail of mahogany Settle
(project on page 46)

in my opinion, flake figure doesn't show up very well when finished light.

Red Oak ▪ This is the oak most commonly used in contemporary oak furniture of other styles and in kitchen cupboards of modern manufacture. It is a serviceable wood and recognizable as oak, but its pore structure is coarser and the grain is "stringy." This means that it will not look exactly like white oak finished the same way. In addition, it does not fume well due to low tannic acid content. However, red oak is readily available and a lot of it is available quartersawn, so it is worth considering. Also, quartersawn red oak tends to show even more flake figure than quartersawn white oak!

Mahogany ▪ Mahogany was another wood used during the Arts and Crafts period. Gus Stickley used it—most of his furniture could be ordered in mahogany. The brothers Greene were also known for using it for their furniture. Its tight grain structure, which lent itself so readily to fine furniture designs in the Colonial and Federal periods, made for elegant and sinuous lines when interpreted by the Greenes using Arts and Crafts and Oriental themes. Nowadays it seems easier to find high-quality mahogany than some domestic hardwoods (like quartersawn white oak) because it doesn't pay to ship and import low-quality wood.

Elm ▪ Elm is softer and easier to work than oak, although it too is coarsely grained, compared to maple, for example. Stickley built some of his early pieces out of elm, and recommended it for woodwork in homes. Its grain can have an attractive feathery pattern, and it can look good finished light or dark. Elm has been largely overlooked as a furniture wood, perhaps unfairly. It is also relatively inexpensive.

This might be a good wood to experiment with. Try some on a small project. Watch whether it ages well, and see if you like the results you get.

Chestnut ▪ Although hard to come by due to chestnut blight and the zeal of tree-service workers who cut down healthy trees, you can find recycled chestnut lumber in the form of old barn and building beams; some will be wormy and some will be worm-free. (You may have to do a bit of looking, and it won't be cheap to use this wood. Your cost will be in purchase price or labor, or both.) This is a pretty wood; it is coarsely textured but easier to work than oak.

Cherry ▪ This wood is being used for Arts and Crafts style furniture today, but was not much used, to my knowledge, during the historic Arts and Crafts period. It may be that lumber supplies for this wood had been virtually logged out by the end of the Victorian period, and the wood now being used is the "renaissance" of commercial production of cherry wood for lumber. Cherry is worth consideration by the woodworker because it is obtainable, attractive, and pleasant to work with. Interestingly, it is not the orchard type of tree that produces commercial cherry lumber.

POSITIONING BOARDS WITHIN A PIECE

After you have purchased your wood and brought it home, your next wood-selection decision will be how best to arrange the boards within a piece of furniture so that the grain of the wood forms an eye-pleasing pattern. Keep the principle of symmetry in mind while attempting this. If you are working with oak, be aware that its strong visible grain can create optical illusions—for instance, the visual impression of sag-

ging boards will give a negative impression. Therefore, be sure to arrange the boards in such a way that the grain will not give that appearance. Grain and ray-flake pattern will be more prominent after finishing, so you must be watchful for effects that may be subtle only on unfinished wood.

Wood selection is an area where you, the individual woodworker, can excel. While I'm not suggesting you try every possible combination, taking some time to arrange the slats in a pleasing pattern is certainly worthwhile. A worker in a furniture factory has to take the pieces off the conveyor belt as they come and doesn't have the luxury of saying, "Hmm...I'll just leave these slats arranged here on the workbench, go out and look at the garden for a while, and then see if I still like the way I placed them." You'll be enjoying this chair or cabinet for years to come, so why not take a little time now to exercise your judgment and good taste?

BOOK-MATCHING

Book-matching derived its name from the practice of selecting adjacent boards as sawn from a log in such a way that they are pulled from the stack and positioned much as one would open a book—the two boards provide a mirror image of the grain pattern (figure 3).

When trying to book-match, something to watch out for is "run-out." This is when the grain runs in one face of the board and out the other. When a board is flipped and book-matched, one face will look lighter, the other darker, depending on the lighting (figure 4, page 30). This will make the wood in your piece look mismatched. It may be one reason Gus Stickley

figure 3

avoided book-matching on early pieces. Later his furniture used veneer for book-matched panels. The reason that adjacent boards may have a light/dark appearance differential is that the saw will cut straight even though the grain may spiral around the tree. Light seems to bounce off some tree structures and be absorbed by others. Run-out is both structural and aesthetic. An extreme example of a problem caused by this important phenomenon occurred when airplanes were first being built and their wooden frames were vulnerable to run-out. Run-out caused some airplane frames to fail in midair.

figure 4

USING "DEFECTS" IN WOOD

According to author William H. Brown, "A defect in wood is any irregularity or imperfection that reduces its volume or quality and in this sense abnormal growth, knots, and insect or fungal attack are all defects." (*The Conversion and Seasoning of Wood*, Linden Publishing, 1988.)

A woodworker can use defects in wood, that is, work them into the design of the furniture—even flaunt them—or avoid them as much as possible. Gustav Stickley wrote of the Japanese woodworker who "regards a piece of wood as he might a picture and his one idea is to do something with it that will show it to the very best advantage, as well as gain from it the utmost measure of its usefulness." If you are working wood, you will want to learn when defects may enhance appearance without compromising the structure and utility of your finished work.

Sapwood ▪ Sapwood is the outer, most recently alive, part of the tree. Sometimes the wood within $\frac{1}{2}$" of the sapwood on a white oak tree will be a lighter shade than the rest of the heartwood when it is fumed with ammonia. Gustav Stickley didn't use sapwood for aesthetic purposes. When he used it, he hid it with aniline dye. Of course, you don't have to follow his lead—you can use sapwood in a creative way. In general, when purchasing boards, you want to buy the ones that are heartwood with very little sapwood. Boards with too much sapwood can be used for cleats or frames covered with upholstery. On quartersawn white oak, sapwood generally has a lighter appearance than heartwood.

Pin Knots and Waves ▪ Like the Japanese woodworker who Gus Stickley mentions, you can use these for aesthetic purposes. If you do so, do it boldly and deliberately—as a focal point. A half-hearted use of such wood will look like an unsuccessful attempt to hide it.

Spalting ▪ These are black lines in the grain of wood caused by fungus and water. Lathe turners use spalting to aesthetic advantage, so you can too. Lightly spalted wood does not pose structural problems. When the spalting is extensive, such wood may be used for panels, but not main structures of furniture.

Caution ▪ Certain wood defects can present problems with structural strength. Knots larger than $\frac{1}{4}$" in diameter should be avoided because the wood around them will be inclined to crack or break. Also, grain extremes—such as wild or curly grain—can make wood more difficult to plane or cut.

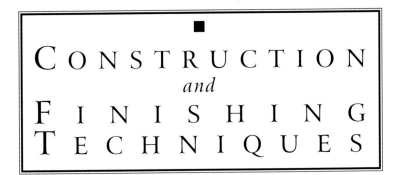

CONSTRUCTION *and* FINISHING TECHNIQUES

Before you start work on a project, it's a good idea to review the topics covered in this section. They include necessary tools, shop safety, Arts and Crafts furniture construction techniques, sanding, finishing options, care of fine furniture, and choosing a first project.

WORKSHOP HAND TOOLS

If your preference or budget doesn't allow use of power tools, here is a list of hand tools most frequently needed for building Arts and Crafts style furniture.

marking gauge (or mortise gauge)
mortise chisel
backsaw (Western or Japanese)
workbench with vise
bar clamps, C-clamps, or rope and wedges
hand plane
square
cabinetmaker's or carpenter's mallet (a ball peen hammer could possibly be substituted)
drill
awl

An awl is handy for making marks (or dents) for drilling holes. It helps to keep the drill from "skating." The marking gauge (or mortise gauge) will not be quite as useful on oak as it is on softer woods. Because of oak's coarse grain, the gauge cutter wants to follow the grain of the wood. You may find yourself using a pencil and straightedge instead.

Note: We have not listed required tools for each of the projects, except for the Knockdown Settle (page 46) and the Large Bookcase (page 133) for which specialized tools are essential.

SHOP SAFETY

I don't just talk about safety, I practice it. Always protect yourself, your family, and your pets. Keep children and pets out of your work area when you are using power tools or potentially toxic finishing products, or when you are generating large amounts of dust.

If you are using power tools, study the safety sections of the owner's manual. Keep your hands away from blades and cutters. Use push sticks, blocks, feather boards, and hold-downs. And think ahead—if your hand slips, will it go anywhere near the cutter? If a piece of board kicks back, where will it fly? Learn how the guards work on your power tools. There are a lot of aftermarket safety options available for table saws and other equipment.

Do not use dull-bladed tools. Most woodworkers who have had accidents in their shops will tell you that they were using a tool that was too dull. When working with

The authors strongly urge readers to follow manufacturer's instructions for safety precautions when using any woodworking tools, particularly power tools, or finish related products, including ammonia. The use of Material Safety Data Sheets, available from product manufacturers, is particularly recommended.

Japanese saw

a hand tool, for example, the tendency is to try to force it. Forcing a tool invites accidents. And, dull power tool blades are more likely to grab or kick back.

Recommended sources for learning hand-tool use are books by Roy Underhill of "The Woodwright's Shop," and these books: *Japanese Woodworking Tools: Selection, Care, and Use*, by Henry Lanz, Taunton Press, and *Japanese Woodworking Tools: Their Tradition, Spirit, and Use*, by Odate Toshio, Sterling Publishing Company.

ARTS AND CRAFTS JOINERY

Mortise and Tenon Variations ■ Gustav Stickley said that in furniture designs that utilize the through tenon, the tenon shows so that "the manner of putting the piece together is both revealed and emphasized." Use of mortise and tenon joinery dates back at least to the ancient Egyptians, and probably predates the invention of the wheel. Although it is the predominant construction method in Arts and Crafts style furniture it is hardly news. It is used, however, to make chairs, tables, cabinet frames—just about any kind of furniture in this style.

Blind Mortise and Tenon

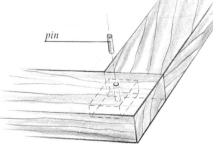

pin

figure 1

The mortise and tenon is a very strong method of joinery. Traditionally, frame and panel construction also relies on mortises and tenons to make the frame. To make mortise and tenon joints by hand you will need these tools: mortise chisel, cabinetmaker's or carpenter's mallet, and a mortise gauge. Constructing these kinds of joints requires practice.

MORTISE AND TENON JOINTS

A mortise is a square or rectangular opening or slot in a board that holds a tenon or mating projection cut into the end of a board. There are three types of mortise and tenon joints used in this book: blind, through, and haunched.

In a blind mortise and tenon joint (figure 1) the end of the tenon is not visible on the outside of the completed joint. With a through mortise and tenon (figures 2 and 3) the end of the tenon not only passes all the way

Through Mortise & Tenon

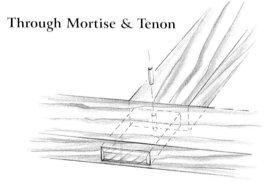

figure 2

through the the mortise, but the end is given a decorative treatment by chamfering (figure 3, page 33).

Tenons are usually cut centered on the end of a board, unless they are haunched. A haunched tenon (figure 4, page 33) is used when the accompanying mortise would be too close to the end of a board to be structurally sound. A haunched tenon allows you to move the joint farther from the end of the board, reducing stress on a structurally weak point. Thus, by moving the tenon to one side the problem is avoided.

Always cut the mortise prior to cutting the tenon. It is easier to trim a tenon to a smaller size than to enlarge a mortise slightly.

Parts of a Tenon
(Through mortise & tenon)

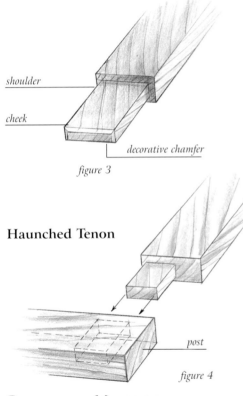

shoulder

cheek

decorative chamfer

figure 3

Haunched Tenon

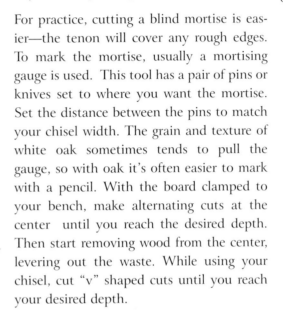

post

figure 4

CUTTING A MORTISE

There are a variety of ways to make a mortise.

By Hand with Chisel and Mallet ▪ This is the least expensive way to make a mortise in terms of tools: there is no lengthy machine setup time. Mark where you want the mortise, and start cutting it. If you have only a few mortises to do, or if you have a number of different sizes to make in the same piece, it might be more efficient to use this method. Besides, you'll have the satisfaction of knowing and bragging that you cut those joints by hand. You get an aerobic workout—without expensive exercise equipment. This technique is proudly referred to as "neanderjoining" in some quarters. (If you want to save time, why not buy the completed piece?)

Chisels

For practice, cutting a blind mortise is easier—the tenon will cover any rough edges. To mark the mortise, usually a mortising gauge is used. This tool has a pair of pins or knives set to where you want the mortise. Set the distance between the pins to match your chisel width. The grain and texture of white oak sometimes tends to pull the gauge, so with oak it's often easier to mark with a pencil. With the board clamped to your bench, make alternating cuts at the center until you reach the desired depth. Then start removing wood from the center, levering out the waste. While using your chisel, cut "v" shaped cuts until you reach your desired depth.

Using a Drill or Drill Press ▪ These tools are used to first remove the wood. Then you follow up with a chisel and mallet to chop the hole into the square or rectangle. You will need a way to keep your drill holes in a straight line, such as by using some sort of fence or fixture.

By Router and Template ▪ You will probably want to use a spiral bit that will pull the chips out of the mortise. It may take a fairly long time to make a mortise with a router because you need to rout the depth in stages. If you try to take too much wood out at one time, the router will kick back and spoil your piece. You could injure yourself as well.

Specialized Mortising Machine or Hollow Chisel Mortising Bit on a Drill Press ■

Setting up whichever machine you are using may take considerable time. You should mortise a test piece to check your setup for accuracy. A hollow chisel mortise bit consists of a square chisel with a drill bit turning in the center of it. You drive the chisel through the wood and the drill bit pulls out the waste. A drawback of most of the chisels is that they may make a round hole of slightly larger diameter than the square chisel, and these holes will need to be cleaned up on any through mortises (figure 5).

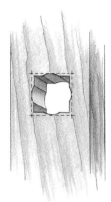

figure 5

This technique is best used, for example, when many mortises must be made in the same piece of wood, such as in a spindle Morris chair. In the latter case, a total of 60 mortises must be cut in four pieces of wood—just for the spindles. The specialized tool allows you to use more leverage than you can get on a drill press, which can be useful in mortising a hardwood like white oak.

TENON CUTTING WITH POWER TOOLS

There are several ways to machine-cut a tenon, but in every way of cutting, you must cut the shoulders on all four faces. Cut them so that your saw kerf goes slightly deeper than the finished thickness of the tenon.

On Your Table Saw in Multiple Passes ■
Make your shoulder cuts. Adjust the height of your saw blade to the amount of wood you want to remove from each side to make the tenon. Test your adjustment with a scrap of wood the same thickness as the board you are trying to tenon. Once you are ready to work on your real tenon, make your first cuts on each face of the board. Now you can check your work by inserting the corner of your unfinished tenon into your mortise to see if the size is all right.

Make successive cuts from your last ones up to the shoulder of the tenon. (Because this method is likely to leave grooves on the face of the tenon, you can leave it a little on the thick side, then sand it with a pad sander or sanding block.) An advantage of this method is that it doesn't require any specialized equipment. A disadvantage is that it can be time consuming.

On Your Table Saw with a Dado Blade ■
With each saw pass you can remove ¾" of wood. You will have fewer passes this way, so it's quicker than using a conventional blade. If ridges result, they will be farther apart.

With a Homemade Tenon Jig and a Table Saw ■ Such a jig should hold the wood vertically so that the sides of the saw blade are cutting the face of the tenon.

With a Commercial Tenon Jig and a Table Saw ■ The commercial jig may be easier to make fine adjustments on, but it also takes a while to set up. For any method other than using hand tools, you should do a test tenon or do the first one oversized and gradually remove more wood until it fits the mortise. Getting the jig set up to exactly the size tenon you want is tricky. A disadvantage of using the boards vertically on a homemade or commercial tenon jig is that you can't work on extremely long pieces that need tenons on both ends (such as the front and back pieces of the settle on page 46).

HAND-CUTTING A TENON

Few woodworkers who own a tablesaw or bandsaw will want to hand-cut tenons, but with a sharp high-quality backsaw, a vise, and a little practice, good results can be achieved in a relatively short time.

Mark the tenon shoulders and draw the cheeks of the tenon on the edges of the board. Draw lines on the end of the board connecting the cheek lines. Cut the shoulders. Using a miter box to start the cuts will help keep them straight. Cut just past the cheek lines you drew.

Mount your board at a 45 degree angle in a vise, and cut on the outside of the cheek lines until you reach the shoulder cuts. Flip the board over and repeat.

Now place the board vertically in the vise and saw between the 45 degree cuts you made. Check the tenon for fit, trimming with a bull-nose plane or a chisel. Then mark and cut the sides of the tenon.

THROUGH MORTISE AND TENON

A through mortise is usually cut from both sides to avoid splitting the wood. If you are cutting a through tenon, you want to bevel the edges with a decorative chamfer. Set your saw blade to a 45 degree angle. (A 30 to 60 degree setting works, depending on what you are using the tenon for, how big it is, and how you want it to look.) You will need to use a stop to cut a uniform bevel on the ends of the tenon. Or, you can use a stationary belt or disc sander to sand the chamfers.

SPLINES AND BISCUITS

Many wood glues tend to act like a lubricant when first applied, allowing boards to slip out of alignment when clamps are applied. Not only do fine joinery methods prolong the service life of a piece of furniture, but they also aid in the gluing process. They align and position component parts, and, to a degree, they strengthen joints.

In Arts and Crafts furniture, biscuits can be used to edge-join boards, but are not appropriate for other joinery. Splines and biscuits are sometimes used to accomplish the same tasks, such as joining boards in a tabletop. Historically, dowels were also used in edge-joining boards, but are seldom used for this purpose today.

SPLINES

Splines are strips of wood that fit into grooves cut into board edges. For the greatest strength, the grain in the splines should run at right angles to the joint, but many old Arts and Crafts furniture pieces use a strip of wood cut from the edge of a board. The splines in many old pieces have come loose due to wood shrinkage.

Many antique Arts and Crafts pieces used a rounded tongue and groove joint to align boards (the round tabouret did, for example). This type of joinery uses a little more wood because of the overlap, and it is more suited to factory furniture methods where machines can be left set up for this purpose.

Splining Boards ■ Cut a matching groove in both boards you want to join together. Use a table saw or a router and a slotting bit. Cut a strip of wood off of a board so that it's wide enough to fit into both of the slots you've cut. Glue the strip into place when you want to glue the joint.

BISCUITS

Biscuits are a relatively modern invention. They are made of compressed cross-grained wood material. The biscuit fits into a recess that is cut with a specialized biscuit cutter or with a slotting bit in a router. Biscuits are designed to swell when glue is applied. Although they do not make an acceptable substitute for mortise and tenon joinery, they can do a very good job of edge-joining tabletops, bookcase sides, and the like. You will not get the decorative effect of a spline, but biscuits are easier to use than splines and are not as difficult to align as dowels. To this end, they are the least work for the home wood-worker, and therefore more likely to bring success.

Biscuiting a Joint ■ NOTE: I recommend biscuits only be used in place of dowels for gluing up tabletops or panels. They are not a replacement for mortise and tenon joinery. Either use a specialized biscuiting tool or joiner, or a slotting cutter of the correct width in your router. Put your boards together and mark where you want the biscuits. (Make sure the slots do not interfere with D-handles or mortises.) Glue and clamp the pieces together with the biscuits. Level and sand the glue off the joint.

CHOOSING DOWELS

If you are trying to find white oak dowels at your supplier, pick up an oak dowel of the appropriate size and try blowing on one end. (I'm serious.) If you can feel air coming out the other end, or can feel air going into the dowel, it's red oak. You can also tell them apart by the pore structure. The ends of red oak dowels tend to look "holey." You may also detect some color difference.

DOWELS

Dowels have gotten a bad name in furni-turemaking, mostly because of their misuse in butt-jointed chair construction. I own some "bargain" chairs that I bought new when I purchased my home ten years ago. They are butt-jointed. I have probably reglued each butt joint twice since I have had the chairs because the joints have the dismaying habit of working apart. (I will be glad to replace these chairs with ones I have made myself.) Dowels work well in edge-joining, but require care in their alignment. A specialized edge-joining dowel jig is recommended if you choose to use dowels for this purpose.

You should keep some dowels around in assorted sizes for pinning mortises. Dowels do this job very well. Even if the glue should fail in pinned mortise and tenon joints, the piece of furniture should still stay together. When mortise and tenon joints are not pinned they are prone to separation. When one of the doors in my 1919 house would no longer close properly, we discovered that its mortise and tenon joints had not been pinned, and one was separating in such a way that the door could no longer fit inside the door frame.

PINNING JOINTS

First drill a hole in a piece of scrap and check that your dowel will fit snugly. Dowels are sometimes undersized, and you may need to use a $1\frac{1}{32}$" drill bit to fit a $\frac{3}{8}$" dowel. Through tenons are usually pinned in the center, while blind tenons are pinned closer to the tenon shoulders. Mark the location for the dowel hole with an awl. Drill a hole so that it will pass through the tenon into the other side of the joint. Put a little glue on the sides of the hole. Drive a dowel into the hole. Cut the dowel off as flush as you can without marring surrounding the wood. Sand flush.

OTHER REQUIRED TECHNIQUES

Here are a number of other important techniques.

CUTTING A DADO

A dado is a slot cut at a right angle to the grain of the wood. If it parallels the grain, it is called a groove. Cutting a dado is a similar operation to cutting a tenon cheek because you can use a dado blade on your table saw to remove up to ¾" of wood. Or you can make many passes with your regular saw blade if you don't have a specialized dado cutter. You can also rout a dado with a router using a jig or guide to cut the proper width.

If you are using only hand tools, you can cut two saw kerfs to approximately the width and depth of the dado, then use a chisel or specialized plane to clean out the waste.

LAYING OUT AND CUTTING CURVES

For laying out small curves, use a compass; for larger curves, use trammel points that clamp to a stick. To cut the curves, use a band saw if you have one. Otherwise, a saber saw can be used, though the cut will be rougher. There are plans available for mounting a saber saw in a table, with ball bearings to guide the cut, which will make the cut cleaner. A scroll saw with a coarse blade could also be used. For hand work, a frame saw can do the job, but requires some practice. Holding the saw properly is important. Clean up the saw marks with a belt sander, drum sander, or wood rasps and files, as well as sandpaper.

GLUING AND CLAMPING

Gluing ■ Originally, hide glue was used in furniture construction, and it's still used today, particularly for furniture restoration. Glue in the form of powder or pearls is soaked in water, then heated in a double-boiler glue pot until it's the consistency of motor oil. Usually, hide glue does not require elaborate clamping.

For edge gluing, use a "rub joint." Put glue on both pieces, slide them back and forth about ½" to 1" to eliminate bubbles, and hold them together for 1 minute. Then set them aside to dry.

One of the big advantages of hide glue is that it's easy to disassemble and reassemble joints when hide glue has been used. Hide glue is therefore important in making musical instruments and chairs with butt-joint or round tenon construction, because that type of chair often works itself apart and needs to be reglued. Because the pinned tenon joinery of Arts and Crafts chairs is not susceptible to working apart, hide glue is not essential for Arts and Crafts furniture construction.

Modern woodworking glues may be used to good advantage in building furniture in the Arts and Crafts style. Avoid glues with a tendency to "creep." (Glues have been rated for their characteristics in *Fine Woodworking*.) Follow the instructions on the bottle for how long to leave your piece clamped.

Clamps ■ A good selection of "C" clamps or hand screws and bar or pipe clamps is necessary for making Arts and Crafts furni-

Rope clamps

ture. If you don't have enough pipe clamps, you can use rope or wedge clamps. The latter is an instrument maker's trick.

SURFACE PREPARATION OF LUMBER

PLANING

White oak is most commonly sold as rough lumber (not even planed on one side), with the original sawmill markings still on the boards. Frequently the wood has surface stains from moisture in the kiln.

Because the condition of the wood is very difficult to assess when the lumber is rough, take along a small block plane to the dealer. If he will let you use it, check the boards you have selected for purchase by planing off a small amount of rough surface near the edge.

Many dealers will do planing for a fee. If your dealer will plane the wood for you, it does save you labor. But, realize that, commonly, planing takes off ⅛" from each face of a board. If you want a full inch-thick finished board, you'll probably need to start with 5/4 rough lumber.

You can hand plane lumber if you like, but it takes a long time. If a board is slightly cupped or warped, you can flatten the board via careful hand planing by removing high spots. If you tried the same procedure with a machine planer, the feed rollers of a power planer will often temporarily flatten a board as it passes through the machine, but it will spring out of shape again as soon as it is out of the planer. A combination of hand and machine planing can be successful in flattening cupped or warped boards.

Planing reduces the thickness of the board and takes off rough saw marks. Finer grained hardwoods such as cherry also require planing. Planer knives will not dull as quickly on softer hardwoods as they do on white oak, however. If your planer has variable speeds, your final pass, at least, should be at the slow speed to get as smooth a surface as possible. Planer marks are difficult to sand out on a relatively hard hardwood like oak.

If your planer tends to "snipe," or remove too much wood at the end of a cut, you may need to count that part of the board as waste. It isn't a bad idea to make projects from a hard but inexpensive wood such as ash until you get to know your equipment. Buy the best equipment that you can afford, but know how to compensate for any deficiencies.

SANDING

One-third of furnituremaking is sanding. If you hate sanding, you had best find another craft. Because sanding may be disagreeable and lengthy, it pays to get high-quality sanding materials.

It's my theory that American Arts and Crafts furniture was designed with machine sanding in mind. Its large flat surfaces certainly lend themselves to machine sanding, but I am not aware how far along mechanized sanding technology had come at the turn of the century.

CONTEMPORARY SANDING MACHINERY

Fortunately, as a modern woodworker, you don't have to do all of your sanding by hand. There are many types of sanding machines available today, including drum sanders, belt sanders, drum thickness sanders, random orbit sanders, pad sanders, and detail sanders.

Drum Thickness Sander ▪ This tool is used to thickness-sand wood, and can be used as a substitute for a planer for very wide boards, but achieves its results much more slowly. This sander doesn't tear out figured grain like a planer would. It can be used to flatten a tabletop. Don't try to remove too much wood at once or you will burn lines into the wood; watch your thickness setting. It's better to remove wood with a series of light passes.

Drum Sander or Drum Sanding Machine ▪ This tool may be used to sand curves, such as arches on furniture, or for sanding corbels. You can get a template drum sander that has a wheel the same diameter as the sanding drum positioned below it. The wheel can ride on a template or guide to sand identical shapes—such as chair parts.

Random Orbit Sander ▪ This can be useful for sanding flat areas quickly. Because these machines often have dust-collection bags, the dust-collection feature makes their sanding action more efficient. You can use this sander on assembled or partially assembled pieces. Follow up with fine sandpaper to remove any swirl marks left from using coarser grades of sandpaper with this sander. Lower quality machines sometimes make more prominent marks.

Belt Sander ▪ This versatile tool can remove planer marks, even out boards, remove coarser sanding scratches, and sand edges of boards or broad curves. Keep it in motion; don't let it sit in one spot or it will sand too deeply (dig a "hole"). With variable speed machines, you can use the low speed with fine-grade sandpapers. This helps avoid burning.

Pad Sander ▪ The quality of pad sanders varies significantly according to the purchase price. Some lower-priced models have a limited life span. Read the model reviews in woodworking magazines. The pad sander's size and weight make it easy to handle, and this is a good all-around tool— useful for household as well as shop. The most common type uses one-quarter of a sheet of sandpaper, and it can get into smaller spaces. It's a good tool to use prior to final hand sanding.

Detail Sander ▪ A detail sander can be used for getting into tight places, close to corners, and sanding between slats or spindles. Price and quality vary. Cheaper ones are more difficult to use due to vibration and noise. Durability is also an issue. If your use is infrequent, an inexpensive model may be acceptable.

By Hand

If you are sanding by hand, probably the most useful technique is to use a sanding block to wrap your sandpaper around. This allows you an even pressure, and helps you to hold onto the sandpaper and get more mileage out of it. There is no substitute for a final hand sanding on fine furniture.

Don't feel that you have to use sanding machinery. Sanding equipment saves time, however, on what many woodworkers feel is a lot of drudgery. If I had to choose between spending money on a specialized mortising machine and on sanding tools, I'd choose the latter. It takes longer to sand than to do joinery and I find joinery more satisfying, so I don't resent the "hands on."

The Ladies' Home Journal
advertisement, 1913

The Ladies' Home Journal
advertisement, 1913

IN GENERAL

Sandpaper quality varies and is of particular importance in furnituremaking. It has improved enormously since turn of the century, but the array of available options is often bewildering. Differences include the type and amount of grit, type of backing material, the type of glue used, and any lubricants that go over the grit to keep it from clogging.

Old-fashioned garnet paper works well for hand sanding. The brittle grit chips and shatters as you sand, creating new abrasive surfaces on the paper. Unfortunately, in a sanding machine, the abrasive is quickly shattered and worn off the paper. Silicon carbide and aluminum oxide are synthetic grits often used for machine sanding, as they are tougher than garnet.

Paper is available in a variety of weights, with the heavier ones suited to hard use. Paper is economical for flat sanding, but when sanding curved surfaces, cloth is more flexible and tougher than paper. Non-clogging papers are great for resinous softwoods such as pine, but aren't necessary for sanding hardwoods such as oak. Change your paper when it stops working efficiently. A lot of time and effort are wasted by trying to squeeze the last bit of abrasive off a piece of sandpaper.

Sandpapers are graded with numbers, with the low numbers for coarse grits and high numbers for fine grits. It usually does not pay to skip grit grades while working on a project, especially when working in oak. Depending on how smoothly you have planed the wood, you want to start out with a #100 or #120 grit and work your way up to #220 by the time you are doing the final sanding in preparation for applying a finish.

Grits finer than #220 aren't usually used on unfinished wood.

Because oak has open pores, it's difficult to see planer marks and sanding scratches when the wood is unfinished. Unfortunately, after the finish goes on, these marks become much more visible. Good shop lighting is a must. Inspect your project before you apply finish by looking at it from a low angle. Good inspection and a thorough sanding regimen are essential for professional results and are the basis of a good finish. After your final sanding, thoroughly wipe off the sawdust from your project with a clean, soft rag. Immediately prior to finishing, clean your project well with a tack cloth. Using the rag first to remove excess dust prolongs the life of your tack cloth.

FINISHING—THE FUMED FINISH AND ALTERNATIVES

Wood finishing is quite subjective. Highly regarded woodworkers and finishing experts will disagree about the aesthetic qualities and even some of the disadvantages of various finishes. The challenge is for the individual to find a method that he or she is comfortable with. There are a number of trade-offs involved because each method has pros and cons.

My own philosophy of wood finishing stems from my background in researching and building historic musical instruments. I am as concerned as a museum curator about whether a damaged finish can be repaired and restored. When I create something that requires planning and hours of labor, it just doesn't make sense to me to use a finish that not only will look bad if damaged, but will be next to impossible to repair.

I realize that not everyone comes to wood-working with the same background and concerns that I have. So, if there is a particular finishing method that you like, try it out on a small piece of white oak or whatever wood you will be using and see what kind of results you get. If you are trying something new with a prepared product such as a stain or varnish, always follow the directions on the package or use another reputable source, such as *Fine Woodworking* magazine articles for tips on how to use a finishing product.

Something to keep in mind—regardless of what kind of finishing product you use—is the fact that, if it's water-based, it will raise the grain and make it necessary for you to sand after the first coat of finish dries.

ADDING COLOR TO A FINISH — ENHANCING THE COLOR OF WOOD

Ammonia Fuming ▪ This process is not for the uncommitted, the impatient, the hurried, or the careless. It should be undertaken ONLY with properly used safety equipment and precautions. Ammonia can permanently injure eyes (blindness) and skin (alkali burns). It can also injure the respiratory and digestive systems. Using ammonia requires protective clothing, tight-fitting goggles (such as swim goggles), and last, but by no means least, a respirator. I use a full-face respirator and heavy rubber gloves, and keep my skin well covered. NEVER fume in an attached garage or anywhere in your home. A detached garage, shed, or your backyard are proper locations for this process. Good ventilation is essential.

The basic principal of fuming involves leaving unfinished white oak furniture in a chamber (such as a specially constructed tent of plastic sheeting) with dishes of 26 percent ammonia for as long as it takes to darken the wood to the color you want it. NOTE: The furniture will stink of ammonia when removed, possibly for days. This may have interesting ramifications for pet owners.

Gel Stains ▪ Gel stains are easy to apply and good for small projects. High viscosity means a gel stain won't run easily. Many major manufacturers of finish products produce gel stains, so they are easy to find. Gels are a good way to produce an even color.

Pigmented Stains ▪ These may be applied with a lint-free rag or a brush (when using an oil-based product, use a natural bristle brush). A light touch will prevent the color from becoming too opaque.

Aniline Dyes ▪ These are what Gus Stickley recommended for coloring sapwood, if you happen to have a little sapwood in your piece that you want to hide. You can also deepen the color with a dye.

FINISHES THAT PROTECT WOOD

Oil Finishes ▪ For amateur woodworkers, an oil finish is unbeatable for ease of application and easy care for the finished piece. If the finish on your piece gets scratched or receives other minor damage after the finish is on it, just apply more finish. With oil finishes, it's easy to avoid brush marks and easy to avoid mistakes. Always be sure to dispose of oily rags properly to avoid danger of fire, and because oil finishes can "seep," remember to let your freshly oiled work rest for a few days on newspaper or plastic sheeting.

The Ladies' Home Journal *advertisement, 1913*

Tung Oil ■ A prepared tung oil finish is easy to apply—just rub on a thin coat and repeat according to product directions. This is a flexible, not brittle finish that some experts say provides some resistance to marring and water stains. Allow each coat to dry for one hour before repeating.

Danish Oil ■ This is a favorite finish of many amateurs. It goes on easily with a rag and is similar to tung oil, but with various added ingredients to make it more durable.

Water-Based Finishes ■ If you have already used water-based finishes and gotten good results, go ahead and use them. If you have not used them, in my opinion, these are a lot of trouble to apply, and I don't feel the results are worth the hassle. Using them correctly involves a lot of dos and don'ts. My other personal objection to them is that they are in their infancy—their track record is not very long compared to that for their finish alternatives. I prefer methods that have been time-tested for decades or even centuries. If you are interested in using them, read extensively about water-based finishes before using! I recommend Chris Minick's articles in *Fine Woodworking*, "Water-Based Finishes," July/August 1991, #89, and "Choosing a Finish," Jan./Feb. 1994, #104.

Shellac ■ A lot of people don't like to use shellac because it dries so fast, which makes it difficult to continue to "work" the finish, unlike rubbing on an oil finish. Shellac is not as hard as the finishes the manufacturers use. Used alone, it's little protection against water and no protection against alcohol. It is, however, environmentally safer than most of its alternatives. I like its aesthetic qualities and the fact that it is reversible (conservator quality).

Because shellac is alcohol based, it's difficult to use in humid conditions (like Midwest summers!). High humidity has a tendency to turn a shellac finish white as it's being applied or within a brief time after application (perhaps in minutes). If this happens, you must strip the shellac off with alcohol and start over. Factory records indicate that Gustav Stickley's finishing department was frequently laid off when the rest of the factory was in production. I theorize that this was in most instances because of humid weather.

Because shellac has a limited shelf life, it's usually best to mix up your own batch with solvent alcohol. Finishing experts recommend that you use a high-quality natural bristle brush to apply it. Shellac has such a fast drying time that this finish is difficult to spray. For advice on applying shellac, I recommend Bob Flexner's *Understanding Wood Finishing* and Michael Dresdner's *The Woodfinishing Book*.

To use a method similar to that used by Gus Stickley's workmen, make a pad similar to a french polishing pad or ball, with cotton cloth inside a square of lint-free cloth, tying it at the top. Dip it lightly in shellac. Tap it on a nonporous surface, such as a jar lid, to distribute the shellac, then pad the shellac onto your piece. Because you are not using oil and pumice like a true french polish, this method is not as difficult to apply.

Lacquers ■ Historically, the term lacquer referred to shellac and other natural organic resin finishes. Nitrocellulose lacquer was developed after World War I in order to dispose of excess explosive materials. It is presently the finish of choice among manufacturers and many professional woodworkers for reasons such as its relatively fast drying time and good application results under various temperature and humidity conditions. It also dries to a hard surface. Lacquer is generally sprayed to avoid brush marks and save on labor. Nitrocellulose lacquer is a synthetic product containing hydrocarbons, and presently many nitrocellulose lacquers are being phased out due to environmental regulations. Other lacquers, which are water based and not as volatile, will still be available.

Varnish ■ At the turn of the century, varnish was used by many manufacturers of Arts and Crafts style furniture. It is a mixture of oil and resins. If you are using varnish, it should be thinned with the product recommended by the manufacturer, if you want to avoid a plastic look. Some of the old-time varnishes were a mixture of shellac and various natural gums and resins. The cheapest varnishes used back then aged very badly. These included "imitation shellac" which had a tendency to "alligator" as it aged. When selecting a varnish, look for an alkyd- (oil) based variety, and don't buy the cheapest one you can find. Look for a trusted name in finishing products.

Polyurethane ■ I do not use it, and I do not recommend it for any wood, even floors. I realize others may have a different viewpoint. I feel that it is very easy to botch the application of polyurethane. Also, once the finish is cured, if it is damaged, the only option for "repair" is to remove it completely (taking a lot of wood with it).

"OWNING UP" TO YOUR WORK

When you complete a piece you should sign and date it. This is the responsible thing to do. I use a wood-burning tool to sign and date my own work on the underside, such as on the bottom of a rung or stretcher. If your work is signed, your heirs can be proud of your efforts when you are gone. Or, if somehow a piece leaves the care of your friends or family, there will be no mistaking the maker's name. Nobody wants to be accused of producing a forgery.

UPHOLSTERY ADVICE

To date, I have had all of my drop seats and back cushions for Arts and Crafts furniture professionally upholstered. Either cotton stuffing or high density (high resilience) foam is okay, but I trust cotton to last a lifetime.

If you are making a mortise and tenon seat frame for a chair, upholstery webbing can be stretched over it to provide comfortable support. The most authentic support is a spring seat, which is more expensive but provides wonderful results. For a settle, a contemporary solution is to build a seat with a ½" plywood base and a foam rubber body. If you are going to do the work yourself, get your hands on a good upholstery book.

FURNITURE CARE

WAXING

I recommend that you complete the finish on your project with a coat of fine paste wax specially formulated for furniture and woodwork. Not only will the wax add a beautiful patina to your work, but it also adds some protection from impact and moisture damage. Later, a new coat of wax will freshen the look of a piece of furniture. Wax "buildup" is a fallacy invented to sell furniture polish.

The Ladies' Home Journal *advertisement, 1913*

(By the way, lemon oil does not come from lemons!) Don't worry about wax. One or two applications a year are fine and will not hurt your piece. Subsequent coats just melt and merge with previous coats, so removing them is unnecessary.

Historically, especially in colonial times and prior, wax was often used alone as a furniture finish. If you like the look of natural wood, a wax finish is an easy option you might want to consider. If you have chosen an oil finish, you may elect to forego the wax in favor of renewing your oil finish with a new coat of the same finish every year or two.

EFFECTS OF TEMPERATURE AND HUMIDITY

Temperature and humidity extremes should be avoided, if possible. If your climate produces below freezing weather in the winter, your home may be dry at that time of year. A humidifier on the same floor as your fine furniture (but not within a few feet of it) may be a good idea to protect it during the dry season and prevent cracks from developing. Avoid placing fine furniture directly over or against a heat source.

Be advised that prolonged exposure to direct sun will lighten a finish. This is something you can take measures to avoid. Conversely, woods or finishes can darken naturally with age.

TROUBLESHOOTING— RESCUING YOUR PROJECT AND FIXING PROBLEMS

Tenon is Too Thin for Mortise ▪ Glue a piece of matching wood onto the cheek. Cut the tenon again when the glue dries.

Can't Find Dowels in the Right Wood, Such as Mahogany or Quartersawn White Oak ▪ Cut a dowel ¼" or ½" shorter than you need. Sink it below the surface of the dowel hole. Use a tapered plug cutter to cut end-grain plugs. Glue the plug into the hole on top of the structural dowels.

Patching a Hole ▪ If you mistakenly drilled a hole all the way through a board or there is an ugly wormhole in a board you must use, here's what to do: Get a tapered plug cutter. Cut a plug out of some scrap that best matches the grain and color of your piece. Drill out the bad spot in your board and glue the plug into the hole. After the glue dries, trim and sand your patch.

To further disguise a problem in a very prominent location, there are irregularly shaped patch cutters available. You can inlay a matching thin piece of wood in the spot. An irregular shape helps to disguise a patch more easily.

Small Dents ▪ Even though white oak is a hard wood, it is possible to dent it with a dropped tool or piece of wood. Dents can sometimes be removed by putting a drop of water on the dent, letting it soak into the wood, then touching the spot with the tip of a clothes iron, soldering iron, or other small heat source. The steam produced will usually swell the wood close to its original position. Using a piece of uncolored poster board or other thin cardboard between the heat source and the drop of water may help prevent discoloration, and trap the steam in the dent for better results.

Glue Spots ■ Leftover traces and spots of glue are notoriously difficult to see—until a piece is finished. Then they are unfortunately all too evident. Although you can scrape off the finish and the glue in an area and refinish the spot, it's best to eliminate the glue before a piece is finished. There are commercial UV glue additives that you can add to your glue to make it glow in ultraviolet light. Using a small fluorescent light, you can locate the glue spots, and sand or scrape them off before finishing takes place.

HOW TO CHOOSE YOUR FIRST PROJECT

Start out with some easy projects that you can complete in a reasonable length of time. You won't get discouraged like you would working on a big, endless project. The relatively fast results you will get from doing the smaller project will give you a lot of confidence and inspiration. A woodturner I know says that she doesn't make furniture because you start out with a pile of boards and it still looks like a pile of boards after days and days of work planing, cutting, and sanding. It's a long time before you have anything that you can assemble. The time you spend sanding may seem interminable. There are long periods of no discernable progress to the untrained eye. If you are working on a piece only a few hours a week, this period seems to go on forever.

When amateurs decide to make something from wood, they often pick the biggest, most impressive, and most complicated project they can. I made that mistake 20 years ago: it was a Renaissance lute!

Making a couple of small utilitarian projects such as a picture frame or bookends will teach you skills that are necessary on larger pieces. Those small projects will give you

Photograph of a Craftsman bungalow from The Ladies' Home Journal, *1909*

badly needed positive reinforcement. You can get experience applying finish on a small bookend with a complex shape, for instance, that you won't get from applying finish to a piece of scrap. You can tell more easily from finishing a small project how much trouble you will have with runs, and whether the finish will go on evenly. It is important to use a product that you can be comfortable with before you tackle that large piece that cost you so much in hours and materials. And if you make mistakes on your small projects, you can probably still use them. You can always relegate a pair of bookends to a room you don't use a lot, but it might be hard to hide a badly made seven-foot settle!

Gradually, you can increase the complexity and difficulty of the woodworking projects you undertake, and eventually you will end up with large impressive pieces of which you can feel justifiably proud.

Dining table, The Craftsman, *September, 1904*

GUS KNOCKDOWN SETTLE

Finished Dimensions:
7'L x 36"H x 33"W

■ ■ ■ *Difficult*

Although this is a large piece of furniture that uses a great deal of lumber, it's a very useful design made more desirable by its knockdown feature. If you plan to use quartersawn white oak, it may be difficult to find a wide enough board for the back. A later version of Gus's design used a 10" wide backboard, so keep this in mind. At the time I was looking for wood for the settle, I didn't have a wide enough piece of oak for this version. However, I like the results I obtained from using mahogany. Because it's 7' long, I can nap comfortably on this couch! For extra style and comfort, I recommend a couple of large throw pillows in material to match the seat. The settle is also a great "canvas" for showing off needlework pillows in period style.

■ Required Techniques

Cutting a through mortise
Cutting a blind mortise
Cutting through and blind tenons
Making leg posts
Making knockdown pins

■ Required Tools

3 bar clamps
Tapered reamer (see photo 5)
Band clamps

■ Cut List

8	Leg halves	38" x 3½" x 1⅝"
1	Upper back rail	86" x 12" x 1½"
1	Lower back rail	86" x 8½" x 1½"
1	Front rail	86" x 6½" x 1½"
4	Side rails	35" x 5 x 1½"
12	Slats	24" x 3" x ½"
14	Knockdown pins	5" x 1" x 1"
2	Seat frame rails	86" x 4" x 1"
2	Seat frame stiles	32" x 4" x 1"

■ Hardware and Supplies

| 1 | Dowel | ⅜" |

Seat support (see figure 1 on page 52)
Upholstery materials

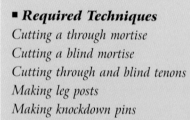

· I N S T R U C T I O N S ·

1

Cut, plane, and square all stock.

LEG POSTS
AND MORTISES

2

Glue each leg post out of two pieces of wood. You may want to use small wire nails as cleats to prevent the halves from moving. Pound two or three nails into one of the pieces, avoiding areas where you will be cutting or mortising later. Cut off the nails so that $1/16"$ projects from the board. Press the boards together so that the projecting nails indent the facing board—this will prevent the boards from slipping out of alignment when they are clamped. Glue the two halves together.

After the glue is dry, trim the glued edges so they are flat and at right angles to the faces. The combined thickness of the glued stock should now be $3\frac{1}{4}"$ halves or $3\frac{1}{2}"$ wide to allow for trimming and squaring up. Trimming can be done on a table saw, jointer, or by hand with a long-bodied plane. NOTE: The sides of the settle posts are not veneered. The glue seams on the settle posts are on the side, not the front.

3

Decide how to orient the posts. Mark all mortise locations; because the upper back of this settle slants for comfort, the mortises for the upper back must slant as well. The tenons for the upper side rails stop at the upper back mortises, so cut the upper side rail mortises as blind mortises. Double-

photo 1: Trimming the settle mortise with a chisel   *photo 2: Trimming the settle mortise with a file*   photo 3

check mortise locations as well as the post orientation before mortising. For cutting mortises, see the photos 1 and 2 and also the instructions on page 33.

SIDE RAILS

4

Cut the tenons on the side rails. For cutting tenons, see the instructions on page 34. I recommend making the rear tenons on the upper side rails the same length as the others, then marking and trimming them to length. Mark and cut the slat mortises.

5

Dry fit the side rails to the posts. Mark the length of the slat shoulders, and cut tenons on the ends of the slats—check for fit. Disassemble (photo 3).

CUTTING TENONS ON THE FRONT, UPPER BACK, AND LOWER BACKBOARDS

6

Because these boards are so long and heavy, it's almost impossible to cut the tenons with a table saw. Cutting with a backsaw is possible, but the tenon may be too wide to cut faces with a normal size backsaw! I suggest using a router and a jig to trim the tenons, taking light cuts (photo 4, page 49.) These tenons should slide easily into the mortises with enough play that they will not seize up in humid weather, but not so loose that they wobble. Mark the tenons so that you will be able to accomplish the knockdown assembly correctly in the future ("Left Front," etc.).

7

Cut chamfers on the ends of the tenons.

8

Cut a decorative chamfer on the top of each post. This is a shallow chamfer about ½" wide, with a flat area in the center. This type of chamfer is usually well rounded, with the crisp edges taken off.

9

Sand all the parts you have made to this point.

10

Glue the slats to the top and bottom rails of the side assemblies, then glue these to the posts.

11

Sand off excess glue when dry.

12

Do a test fitting of the side assemblies with the front, and upper and lower backboards. Trim the tenons as necessary.

MAKING KNOCKDOWN PINS USING A TAPERED REAMER AND A LATHE

13

First you need to make a test "form." Take a block of scrap the same thickness as the settle leg posts and drill a hole slightly smaller than the largest diameter of the reamer, about 1" deep (photos 5 and 6).

14

Finish drilling with a drill bit that is slightly smaller than the smallest diameter of the reamer. Drill all the way through.

15

Put the block into a vise and turn the reamer into the wood. (You can use a wrench to help turn it.) Back it out and clean off the shavings as frequently as necessary. When the small end of the reamer emerges from the far end of the block, stop.

16

Cut the block in half so that you get a longitudinal cross section of the reamer hole. You can use this cross section to check the taper and diameter of the pins you make on the lathe. To check, make sure the lathe is stopped, and hold up your cross section to the pin in progress (photo 6). You should be able to make your pins out of the same lumber you are using for the settle.

photo 4

photo 5

photo 6

17

Make a couple of extra pins while you are at it, in case of loss or damage.

DRILLING HOLES FOR KNOCKDOWN PINS WITH A TAPERED REAMER

18

Mark the positions on the leg posts for the holes for the knockdown pins.

V
BUILDING ARTS & CRAFTS FURNITURE

The Grove Park Inn (1913, Fred L. Seely) is the most well-preserved example of a public Arts and Crafts building in America. Conceived and constructed at the peak of the American Arts and Crafts movement, it reflects the organic style of architecture heralded by practitioners such as Frank Lloyd Wright. In its honest construction and use of natural materials of the region, it puts into practice the main principles of the movement. The furniture, textiles, and lighting fixtures are true to the period, and the Arts and Crafts style has been carefully preserved and restored in the main building.

The Knockdown Settle looks right at home in The Grove Park Inn, located in Asheville, North Carolina.

V

GUS KNOCKDOWN SETTLE

19

Clamp the settle together with band clamps.

20

Drill holes for the pins, starting each hole with a larger diameter bit, then switch to a smaller diameter bit that you can drill all the way through. Carefully use the reamer to cut the taper of each hole. Check for pin fit as you go.

21

Make cleats for the front and back of the seat, and screw them to the inside of the frame. You should make additional cleats that you will set perpendicular to the ones that you attach to the front and back lower rails (figure 1). As the settle can seat several people, the seat support structure is important in order to support their weight.

FINAL STEPS

22

Make a seat frame for the upholstery, using haunched tenons on the end pieces, and allowing ¼" all around for upholstery thickness.

23

Do a final sanding in preparation for adding your finish.

ASSEMBLY ADVICE

Based on my own experience with this settle, it is best to assemble it on its side. Having one or two helpers for assembly is a good idea. Another hint is making sure that settle tenons and pins are well waxed.

24

Set one side assembly on a well-padded floor. Put down extra padding to cushion the through tenons.

25

Put the long rails in their mortises, oriented correctly. Pin loosely.

26

For the tenons that are now in the air, pad the tops of the tenons with soft rags and place the other side assembly on top. Remove the padding from the tenons and guide the tenons into the mortises. Pin loosely.

27

Carefully lower the settle to its upright position. Tighten the pins.

28

To remove the pins in the future, tap them out with a dowel from the small end of the hole.

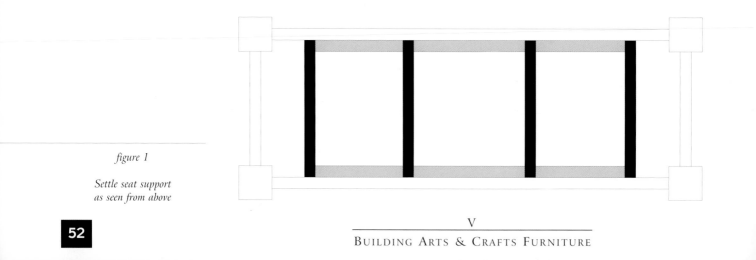

figure 1

*Settle seat support
as seen from above*

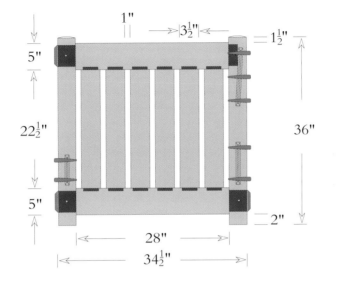

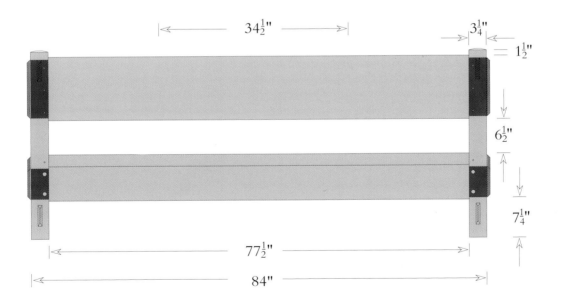

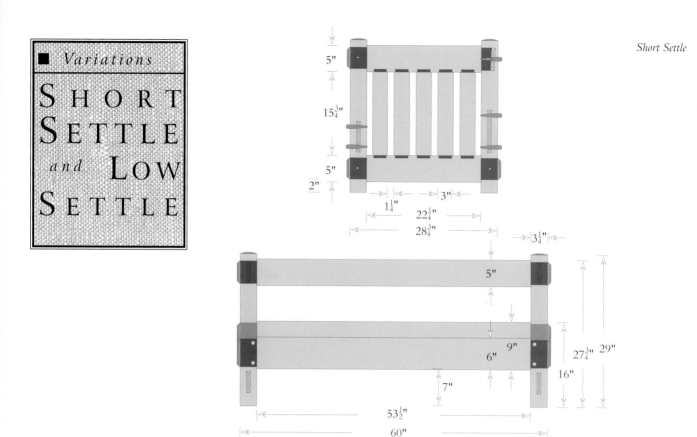

Short Settle

5"

$15\frac{3}{4}$"

5"

2"

$1\frac{1}{4}$"

3"

$22\frac{1}{4}$"

$28\frac{3}{4}$"

$3\frac{1}{4}$"

5"

$27\frac{3}{4}$" 29"

6" 9"

16"

7"

$53\frac{1}{2}$"

60"

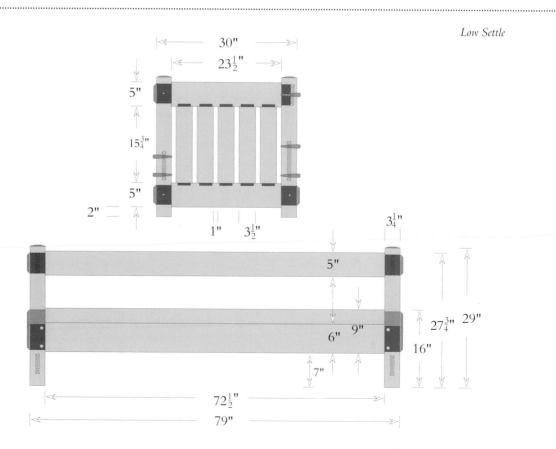

Low Settle

30"

$23\frac{1}{2}$"

5"

$15\frac{3}{4}$"

5"

2"

1" $3\frac{1}{2}$"

$3\frac{1}{4}$"

5"

$27\frac{3}{4}$" 29"

6" 9"

16"

7"

$72\frac{1}{2}$"

79"

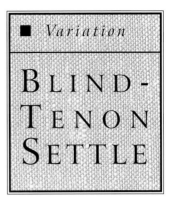

Gus made settles similar to these designs, but without the knockdown feature. Whether or not you incorporate this feature is your choice. Some of Gus's later designs were made with blind mortise and tenon joints throughout, a feature that simplifies their construction. The easier to build blind-tenon settle illustrated below cannot be disassembled. Check your door widths and make sure it can leave your shop!

V

This small table sold well for Gustav Stickley, and several versions were always featured in his later catalogs. Some had wedged through tenons with posts projecting through mortises in the tabletop. Others had through tenons where the lower stretchers projected through mortises in the posts. Finally, there was a version (shown here) with blind tenons throughout. One wonders if Gus found the public unwilling to pay for elaborate joinery. This is a very simple, clean looking design which will be ornamented by your excellent wood selection and finish. The sizes I have provided here should be handy for holding a lamp or a plant, or for displaying metal or pottery vessels. This is a very good first project for perfecting your skill at hand-cutting mortises with a chisel.

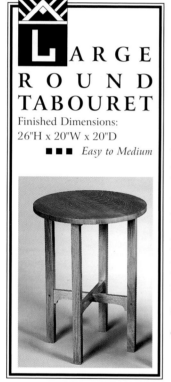

LARGE ROUND TABOURET

Finished Dimensions:
26"H x 20"W x 20"D

■ ■ ■ *Easy to Medium*

■ *Required Techniques*

Cutting a blind mortise
Cutting blind tenons
Biscuiting a tabletop
Doweling joints
Cutting lap joints

■ *Cut List*

4	Posts	26" x 1½" x 1½"
2	Lower stretchers	18" x 2½" x ¾"
2	Upper stretchers	18" x 1½" x ¾"
1	Top	20" x 20" x 1"
		(glued up from smaller boards)*

*You will need enough 5/4 wood to make a 20" diameter top. How much lumber you need depends on the size of the boards available. When you shop for lumber, take along either a copy of the measured drawing or else a 20" paper circle pattern.

■ *Hardware and Supplies*

Dowels	⅜" (enough to pin 6 joints)
Wood screws	1¾" (to countersink)
Table irons	Optional: if desired, use with ¾" screws instead of the longer ones

1

Cut, plane, and square all stock, leaving the posts about 1" over length; they will be cut to length after the mortises are cut.

GLUING UP THE TOP

Original factory versions of the table had a rounded tongue and groove joint to join the boards to make the top. Home workers would have used dowels.

2

Biscuits are an acceptable modern way to align and join the top. You may use this method to join the boards in your top. For biscuiting information, see pages 35-36.

3

Once the glue has dried, flatten the top by planing or sanding it.

4

Cut the top roughly into a circle by using a band or jigsaw. For a perfectly circular top, use a router and trammel arrangement to trim it.

POSTS

5

Determine which face on each post should be positioned outward, then mark where the blind mortises will go for the top and bottom stretchers, remembering to leave extra wood at the top of the posts. The top tenons are "haunched" or set to one side. Haunched tenons are used because if the mortise was too close to the end of the post, it might split.

6

Cut tenons on the ends of the top and bottom stretchers so that they fit into the mortises.

7

Trim the legs to length.

BASE

8

Mark and cut slots for the lap joints where the top and bottom stretchers cross. Cut the decorative curve on the bottom stretchers. Clamp the stretchers together parallel. Sand them even. Test fit stretchers and legs together. Each lap joint is like two "U"s with the open sides fitted together (interlocking) (photo 1).

photo 1

9

Glue each set of stretchers into an X shape. An option that you may choose is to reinforce the joint with a dowel passing vertically through the center of the X.

10

After the glue in the joints dries, glue opposing pairs of legs onto stretchers, mak-

V

LARGE ROUND TABOURET

ing sure they are oriented so that the stretchers are positioned properly. Glue one pair of legs at a time.

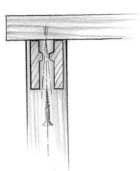

11

Pin the joints with dowels on top and bottom stretchers. For pinning information, see page 36. When the glue dries, clean up the remaining glue. Sand the base well.

figure 1

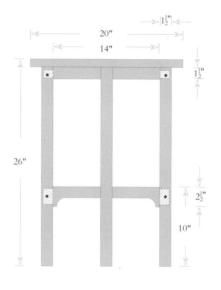

Large Round Tabouret

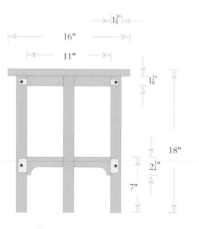

Small Round Tabouret

ATTACHING THE TOP TO THE BASE

Most of the manufactured tables designed by Gus Stickley used figure eight-shaped table irons. In a piece as small as this tabouret, I think it's easier to attach the top directly. If you prefer to use table irons, see how they are attached on page 128.

12

The easiest way to attach the top to the base is to drill countersunk holes through the top stretchers and run screws into the tabletop–1 screw per stretcher (figure 1). Mark and drill pilot holes on the top stretchers for the screws for the top. Do your preliminary sanding.

13

Because you don't want the holes in the top to go all the way through, drill in the following manner: Put the top upside down on your bench or another horizontal surface. Position the base assembly so it's lined up and centered (as in the finished table). Use an awl or a nail to mark pilot holes. Tap the awl with a hammer to leave a dent.

14

Drill the holes; if you're using a hand-held drill, use a stop collar to limit the depth of the hole. If you use a drill press, use the stop on it.

15

Select screws to attach the top that are shorter than the thickness of the tabletop. Temporarily attach the top.

16

Disassemble and do a final sanding. Your project is ready to finish.

With careful wood selection and finish, the smaller version of the round tabouret can be a little jewel. The legs on this piece are proportionately a little bit thicker than on the 26" version (see page 56) but that doesn't hurt its aesthetic qualities.

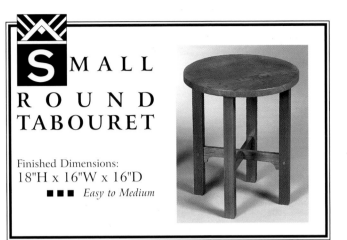

SMALL ROUND TABOURET

Finished Dimensions:
18"H x 16"W x 16"D
■ ■ ■ *Easy to Medium*

- ### Required Techniques
See the 26" version on page 56.

- ### Cut List

4	Posts	19" x 1⅜" x 1⅜"
2	Lower stretchers	15" x 2¼" x ⅝"
2	Upper stretchers	15" x 1¼" x ⅝"
1	Top	16" x 16" x ⅞" (glued up from smaller boards)*

*You will need enough 5/4 wood to make a 16" diameter top. How much lumber you need depends on the size of boards available. When you shop for lumber, take along either a copy of the measured drawing or a 16" paper circle pattern.

- ### Hardware and Supplies

Dowels	⅜" (enough to pin 6 joints)
Wood screws	1½" (to countersink)
Table irons	Optional: if desired, use with ¾" screws instead of the longer ones.

∎ INSTRUCTIONS ∎

The instructions for building this table are identical to those for the 26" version on page 57. The measured drawing is on page 60.

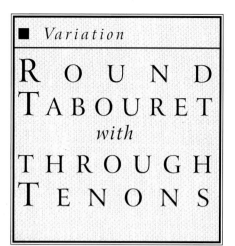

■ *Variation*

ROUND TABOURET
with
THROUGH TENONS

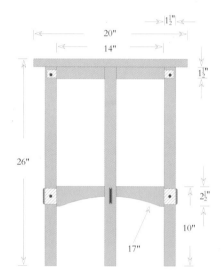

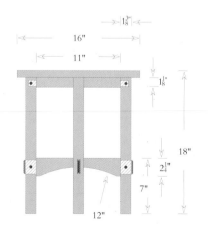

■ **Required Techniques**

Cutting a dado

Cutting a cutout

■ **Cut List**

1   Board   20" x 5" x ¾"

OR

Smaller pieces to yield 2 parts 6½" x 5"
and 2 parts 3½" x 5"

■ **Hardware and Supplies**

4   #8 1¼"-long screws

2   3" x 4" pieces of Formica or sheet metal
     *for the "feet" (If you're using sheet
     metal, you must file the edges of the feet
     so they're not sharp.)*
     *Felt or stick-on pads (Padding the bot-
     toms prevents bookends from scratching
     furniture.)*

Bookends are handy to have around, and they make a nice accent if you are trying to achieve an Arts and Crafts look. There were many shapes of bookends made at the turn of the century. Manual-training students were encouraged to create their own designs. This D-handle pattern is one that I designed for this book to harmonize with the book rack (page 78) and the magazine stand (page 93). This is a great project for trying out finish techniques, and a good first project for the beginner for practicing cutting and working with wood. It uses very little lumber, and you can even use up leftover lumber.

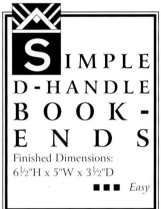

SIMPLE D-HANDLE BOOK-ENDS

Finished Dimensions:
6½"H x 5"W x 3½"D

■ ■ ■ *Easy*

photo 1

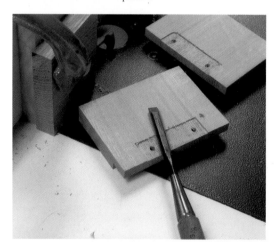

photo 2

1

Cut a board roughly to size, then plane and square it. If you cut your bookends out of one board, the grain will match.

2

Choose your bookend shape.

3

Mark the center of your board.

4

Mark where the dados go (figure 1) and cut them (figure 2 and photo 1). For information on cutting dados, see page 36.

5

Cut the entire board in half (figure 3).

6

Cut bottoms from the side pieces so that the dados are on the 3½" pieces (figure 4).

7

Cut out the "D"-shaped cutouts and the curved corners. Sand (figure 5).

8

Flip the bottoms over and cut shallow recesses for the metal or Formica feet with a router or chisel (figure 6 and photo 2).

9

Drill and countersink the screw holes (figure 6 and photo 2).

10

Glue up the pieces. Use the screws to clamp (figure 7).

11

Make the 2 feet. NOTE: If you use Formica, you can use your table saw to cut them; you may need to clamp a piece of wood to your fence because Formica is thin.

12

Remove the screws and attach the feet through the same screw holes.

13

Remove the feet. Do a final sanding. Your bookends are ready to finish.

14

When the finish is dry, reassemble the bookends.

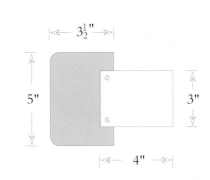

3½"

5"

3"

4"

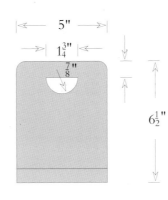

5"

1¾"

⅞"

6½"

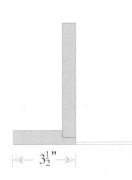

3½"

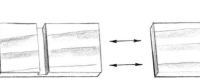

figure 1

figure 2

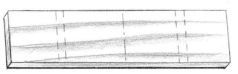

figure 3

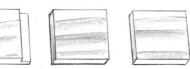

figure 4

figure 5

figure 6

figure 7

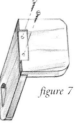

⅞"

DINING *or* SIDE CHAIR

Finished Dimensions:
37"H x 17"W x 18"D

■ ■ ■ *Difficult*

A different design of this chair from The Craftsman

This is one of the most challenging projects in this book. It is one of the most delicate furniture designs from the Arts and Crafts period in America. It and its armchair variation were featured in *The Craftsman*.

■ Required Techniques

Steam bending
Cutting blind mortises and tenons
Cutting angled tenons
Cutting decorative chamfers
Tapering posts
Pinning joints
Cutting arches

■ Cut List

2	Back posts	40" x 2⅜" x 1¼"
2	Front posts	17½" x 1¼" x 1¼"
1	Front arched rail	17" x 3¼" x ⅞"
2	Side arched rails	16" x 3¼" x ⅞"
1	Back top rail	14" x 3¼" x ⅞"
1	Bottom front rail	17" x 1¼" x ⅝"
1	Bottom back rail	14" x 1¼" x ⅝"
2	Bottom side rails	16" x 1¼" x ⅝"
2	Curved horizontal back slats	19" x 1½" x ⅝"
3	Vertical back slats	15" x 2" x ⅜"

■ Additional

4	Cleats	6" x 2½" x ¾" or ⅞"

■ Frame for drop seat

2	Sides	14" x 3" x ⅞"
1	Front	16" x 2" x ⅞"
1	Back	14" x 2" x ⅞"
	Dowels	⅜"

■ Hardware and Supplies

4	Wood screws for cleats	3"
8	Wood screws for cleats	1¾"
4	Wood screws to hold drop seat	1¼"

Upholstery materials

1

Cut, plane, and square all stock. NOTE: When you cut out the horizontal back slats that must be bent, you need to cut them several inches longer than their finished size. Don't cut the tenons on these slats until they are steam bent.

BACK LEGS

As this is a relatively complex design to construct, I recommend that you make a template for cutting out the back legs (photo 1).

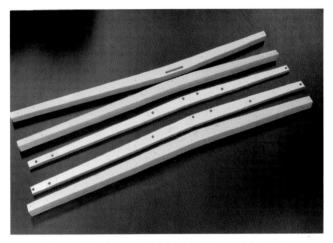

photo 1: Templates and legs for Side Chair and Armchair

2

Draw a rectangle 38" long x 3" high on heavy paper, poster board, fiber board, or plastic. Starting at the lower left-hand corner, measure up 1". From that point, draw a line diagonally to a point 21" to the right, at the top of the box.

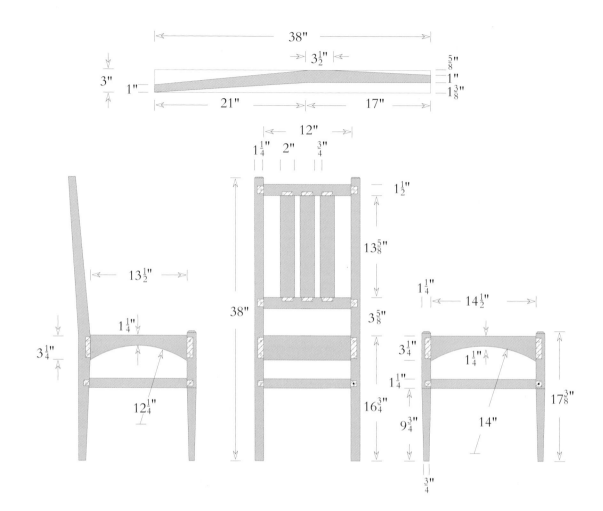

3

Continue the line 3½" to the right, along the top of the box. From that point, draw a line to the right side of the box, ⅝" down from the top of the box. Draw a line down the right side of the box, 1" long (this point is 1⅜" up from the bottom of the box). Draw a horizontal line 17" long to the left, still 1⅜" from the bottom of the box.

4

Transfer this shape to a piece of plastic or other material that you would like to use for a template. Note that when you cut out the leg, the stock needs to be only 2⅜" wide.

There are two ways to shape the back legs: a) mark around the template, cut out and sand, or b) drill screw holes in the template where mortises will be, and above the top and below the bottom of the leg. Screw the template to the leg as above, using a template sanding drum to do final shaping. NOTE: The template will need to be flipped when you are working on the opposite leg, because the mortises in the legs are blind mortises.

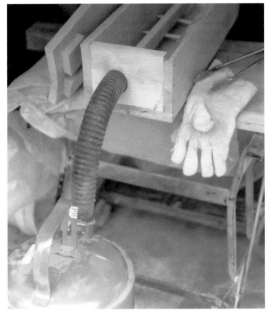

photo 2

BENDING THE BACK-REST PIECES

5

You need to make a two-part bending form for the chair's horizontal back slats. Because I was making a set of chairs, I made my form wide enough to clamp 2 pieces side by side. Laminate enough plywood or other stock to get your width on the form, and enough thickness that both parts will stay together. Band-saw a 24" radius curve for the form.

To bend the horizontal back slats, you can steam or boil them. For either method, it also helps to soak your chair parts overnight in water before "cooking."

STEAMING

6

For my steaming setup, I used a propane cooker, a NEW gas can that never held gasoline, a piece of old radiator hose, and a box built out of scrap (photo 2). Get the water boiling vigorously before putting the horizontal back slats in the box. I used some small scrap pieces to elevate the wood from the floor of the box. The usual rule is to steam wood 1 hour per inch of thickness, so I waited about 40 minutes for each set. (Steaming for too long increases the chance of breakage.) Wearing thick insulated gloves (the wood is 212°F, of course), I pulled the slats out of the box and quickly hand-bent each one over the form (photo 3). They bend best within 20 seconds of being taken out of the steam. After I held the wood on the form for several minutes, I clamped it between the two halves of the form, and started steaming the next pair. It's a good idea to have a couple of duplicate parts made, in case one breaks.

photo 3

BOILING (ALTERNATE PROCESS)

To boil pieces, I used an old, enamel refrigerator drawer that I placed on a burner on the kitchen stove. I boiled pieces for about as

photo 4

long a time as I steamed them. Then, I bent them over the form as I explained above. Either way, after the pieces have dried on the forms overnight, they will have sprung back slightly, approaching a 36" radius.

CUTTING TENONS ON THE CURVED BACK SLATS

7

I cut a piece of scrap to match the curve, and used it to hold the bent pieces while cutting the tenons on the end of the bent horizontal back slats (photo 4).

LEGS AND RAILS

8

Cut the front legs, but do not taper them yet.

9

Decide how to orient the legs, and cut all the ⅜" mortises in the legs.

10

Cut the tenons on the lower back rails to match the lengths of the curved rails.

11

Cut the tenons for the front rails and test them for fit.

12

Cut mortises for the slats in the curved rails.

13

Dry-assemble the curved slats to the back-rest. Use the distance between the curved slats to mark the distance between the shoulders on the vertical slats. Then, cut the tenons on the vertical slats.

UPPER SIDE RAILS

14

The side rails are angled outward about 5½ degrees. This makes cutting the tenons more difficult. Mark which faces of the boards you want on the outside and trim the boards to 15½" in length.

15

Draw the arch on the bottoms of the side boards. Decide which boards will be on the left side (as you face front) and which will be on the right.

16

Cut the top side rails, starting with the arched ones—because of the difference in thickness and the angle of the back leg.

17

Set your table saw to a 5½-degree angle.

18

With your miter gauge on the right side, take the left board with the arch facing toward the gauge fence, and set the stop to cut a shoulder face 1" in from the end (photo 5).

19

After cutting the shoulder, flip the board end for end, with the arch still facing the fence, and cut a shoulder on the opposite side.

20

Cut the left top board.

21

With the same machine settings, take the right board with the arch facing away from the fence. Cut the shoulders, flipping the board as you did for the opposite side, keeping the arch facing away from the fence.

22

Move the miter gauge to the left of the blade. Take the left top board and set the stop on the table saw setup so that the blade is aligned along the same angle of the previous shoulder cut. Cut the shoulder opposite the one you cut in the first step. Again, the arch should face the fence (photo 6).

23

With the same settings, cut the remaining right-side shoulder, again with the arch facing away from the fence.

24

Set the saw blade back to 90 degrees. Angle the miter gauge (still to the left of the blade) to 5½ degrees, angling away from the blade. Align the stop so that the blade will cut a notch in the edge of the board connecting both face cuts.

25

Cut the edges of the left boards, with the arch facing up (photo 7, page 72).

photo 5

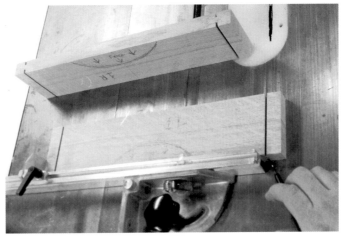

photo 6

26

Cut the edges of the right boards, with the arch facing down.

27

Move the miter gauge to the right of the blade, angle the gauge to the opposite angle, again at 5½ degrees.

28

Cut the left boards with the arch facing down (photo 8, page 72).

photo 7

photo 8

29

Cut the right boards with the arch facing up.

CUTTING THE TOP-RAIL TENON CHEEKS

30

Angle your tenon jig 5½ degrees to the left (OR, your saw blade 5½ degrees to the right).

31

Put the left upper rail on the jig with the arch facing the front of the saw. Raise the saw blade until it just contacts the previously cut shoulder. Move the tenon jig so that you will eventually produce a ⅜" tenon, centered on the board. Cut the first face.

32

Flip the left board to cut a cheek on the other end, again with the arch facing the front of the saw. Cut that cheek.

33

Put the right upper rail on the jig with the arch facing the back of the saw. Cut.

34

Flip the right board with the arch still facing the back of the saw. Cut the 4th cheek.

35

Remount the left board with the arch facing the front of the saw (if you angled the saw blade, you may need to reduce the depth of the cut 1/16"). Adjust the jig to produce a ⅜"-or-more-thick tenon. Cut the other side. Check for fit in the mortise and adjust the jig as necessary.

36

Flip the left board with the arch facing front. Cut.

37

Mount the right board with the arch facing rear. Cut.

38

Flip the right board with the arch facing rear. Cut.

39

Cut the sides of the tenon with a table saw, band saw, or handsaw.

LOWER SIDE RAILS

40

Follow the same procedure used above for the lower side rails. Because they are a different thickness than the top rails, they need to be cut separately, otherwise the tenons will be too thin.

41

The rear tenons are further complicated by the backward angle of the rear legs. Mark the shoulders of the rear tenons all the way around to double check your saw settings.

FRAME ASSEMBLY AND COMPLETION OF THE PROJECT

42

Miter the tenons on all of the rails.

43

Test fit all the parts and trim as necessary (photo 9).

44

Cut decorative chamfers on top of all 4 posts.

45

Taper the front posts, using a tapering jig or a jointer (photo 10).

46

Cut and sand the arch on the side and front rails.

47

Optional: remove ½" to ¾" from the bottoms of the rear legs to give the chair a backwards slant. You may wait until the chair is glued up to do this, if you wish.

48

Sand all of the parts you have made to this point.

photo 9

photo 10

49

Glue the vertical slats to the curved horizontal back slats.

50

Glue the back together. Pin the joints with dowels. Trim and sand flush.

51

Glue the front together. Pin the joints with dowels. Trim and sand flush (photo 11, page 74).

photo 11

photo 12

52

Glue the side rails to the front and back. Pin the joints with dowels. Trim and sand flush.

53

Make a mortise and tenon seat frame, with haunched tenons (photo 12).

54

Make 4 triangular cleats to fit inside the corners of the seat. Predrill, glue, and screw into the chair frame in a location low enough inside the chair that the upholstered seat frame will be recessed.

55

Sand and finish.

56

Upholster with a drop seat over your frame.

Advertisement from The Ladies' Home Journal, *January 1, 1911*

ARM-CHAIR

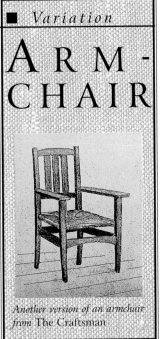

Another version of an armchair from The Craftsman

This variation on the dining/side chair can provide additional seating for the dining room or elsewhere in the home. The armchair seat is larger than that of the dining chair, and this along with the armrests, provides more comfortable seating for longer periods. The addition of the relatively wide armrests also make this design look more massive than its smaller companion chair.

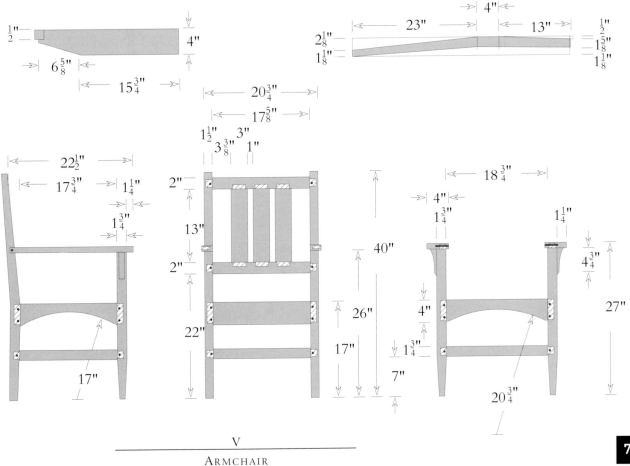

THROUGH-TENON PICTURE FRAME

Finished Dimensions:
19"L x 16½"W

■ ■ ■ *Easy*

This project is easy compared to many in the book because the design is so simple. It can easily be adapted to make a smaller or larger frame. In terms of durability, this design is far superior to most frames with mitered corners. It is also more aesthetically and visually interesting because the verticals are thicker than the horizontals, which creates shadows that accent the joinery.

The sample frame I give instructions for will fit a piece of art work or mat that measures 11"H x 14"W.

Etchings by Phillip C. Thompson

■ ***Required Techniques***

Cutting a through mortise
Cutting a through tenon
Doweling joints

■ ***Cut List***

| 2 | Vertical sides | 16½" x 2½" x ⅞" |
| 2 | Horizontal sides | 19" x 2½" x ¾" |

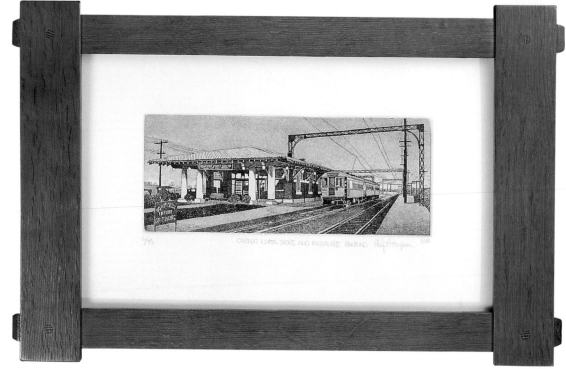

· I N S T R U C T I O N S ·

1

Decide what size frame you want, allowing for a mat and a piece of glass. The completed frame will have a ⅜"-wide rabbet around the inside edge. The inside opening of the frame will be ¾" smaller in each direction than the mat.

2

Decide how wide your horizontals and verticals will be. Cut the pieces to length allowing for the length of the tenons on the horizontals. The verticals will project about ½" beyond the horizontals.

3

Mark and cut the mortises in the verticals, then clean them out. If you are using horizontals and verticals of different thicknesses, position the mortises closer to the back so that they will line up with the centered tenons.

4

Cut the tenons.

5

Test the fit of the joints.

6

Mark and cut decorative chamfers on the edges of the tenons.

7

Sand.

8

Glue the joints together.

9

When the glue is dry, pin the joints with dowels.

10

Using a piloted rabbet bit (preferably mounted in a router table), cut the ⅜" rabbet on the back of the frame by making several shallow cuts to avoid kickback. Because rabbet corners are rounded, use a chisel to cut right angle corners so the glass will fit.

11

Make pilot holes where you want the hanger screws to go.

12

Do the final sanding. Your piece is ready to finish. Remember to have your glass, mat, and other framing materials cut to size AFTER your frame is completed!

■ *Variation*

You can make your frame sides all from the same thickness of lumber. The project will be a little easier to make, but will not be quite as visually interesting.

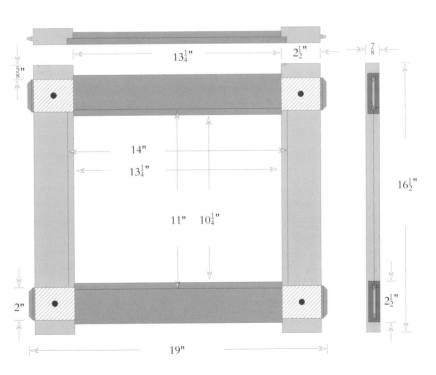

**GUS
D-HANDLE
BOOK
RACK**

Finished Dimensions:
30"W x 31"H x 10"D
■ ■ ■ *Medium*

Another design from *The Craftsman*, I especially like the pretty scrolled arch detail on the bottoms of the side pieces. Gus made a number of D-handle designs that he featured in his catalogs. This is another deceptive piece; while it's true you can't sit knick-knacks on the "V" or trough-shaped shelves, you certainly can store a lot of books. If you're like me and always have more books than places to keep them, a book rack can come in really handy. The D-shaped handles make it easy to move, too.

This 1912 Arts & Crafts home
is located in the old West End
National Register of Historic
Districts in Toledo, Ohio.

■ Required Techniques

Cutting a through mortise
Cutting through tenons
Cutting holes and scrolls
Cutting an interlocking joint
Biscuiting a joint
Doweling joints

■ Cut List

2	Sides	32" x 10" x ⅞" or 1"
4	Shelves	32" x 6" x ¾"
	Dowels	

1

Cut, plane, and square all stock.

2

Glue up the wood for the book rack sides, if necessary. If gluing up, use biscuits or dowels to join boards. Take care to place your biscuits or dowels where they will not interfere with the D-handle or the mortises for the shelves.

3

You will want to cut out the D-handle and the scrolled arch at the same time. Make a template for each of these (photo 1).

4

Note where the mortises will go. For angled mortises, it would be difficult to use a spe-

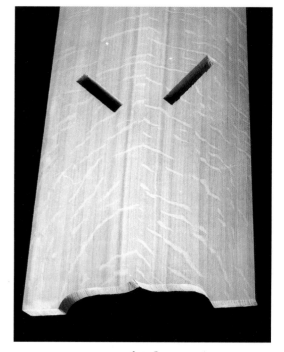

photo 2

cialized mortising machine because of the angle and width of the mortise, so you'll need to use a chisel, or a router and template. If you are doing the latter, make yourself a template.

5

Attach the templates to the book rack side with screws positioned where the mortises will be. Cut out the shapes with a router and sleeve using successive light cuts (photo 2). (A home woodworker of the past would have used a drill to start the hole along with a coping saw.)

6

Do the other side.

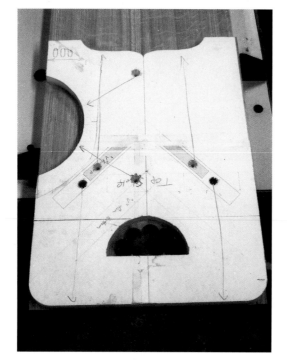

photo 1

photo 3

photo 4

photo 5

7

Cut the angled mortises through the sides (photo 3).

8

Use a doweling jig to drill the holes through the book rack sides for pinning the shelves. It is important to drill these holes straight. Shelves will be in the way once the piece is assembled, so by drilling the holes before assembly, you have eliminated that problem.

9

SHELVES

a) On 2 of the boards, make a ⅜"-wide, ⅜"-deep groove, ⅜" from the edge of the board with a dado blade on your tablesaw (photo 4).

b) Take the other pair of shelf boards. Make a cut so that there is a ⅜" x ⅜" tongue sticking out long ways from the edge of the board. Test fit this joint (see photo 5).

c) Trim boards so that both halves of the "V" are of equal length.

d) Cut the shoulders of the tenons on the ends of the shelf boards. Cut the tenon cheeks so that they fit into the mortises. For information on cutting tenons, see page 34.

d) Glue the 2 shelves into "V's" making sure that they are at right angles. Clamp.

e) After the glue dries, set the book rack sides down on the workbench. Set the shelves over the mortises. Mark where the edges of the tenons should be cut. Do it carefully. If necessary cut them oversized and trim them to fit (This step is the most difficult, and is the reason why this project is not "easy.")

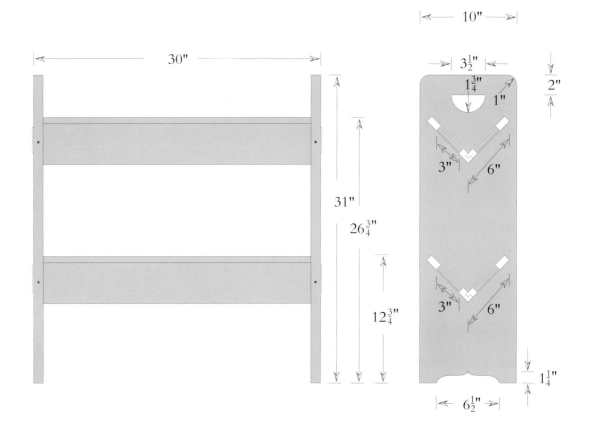

10

Once you have all of the tenons fitted into mortises, cut decorative chamfers on the ends of the tenons. For information on cutting decorative chamfers, see page 32.

11

Sand all parts.

12

Glue the sides to the shelves. Clamp. For information on gluing and clamping, see page 37.

13

After the glue dries, and using the holes you just drilled as guides, finish drilling through the shelf tenons.

14

Pin with dowels, and glue.

15

After the glue is dry, cut the dowels flush and sand.

16

Do final sanding. Your piece is then ready to finish.

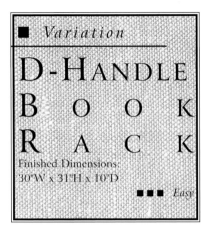

■ *Variation*

D-HANDLE
B O O K
R A C K

Finished Dimensions:
30"W x 31"H x 10"D

■ ■ ■ *Easy*

The variation is less difficult to build. This book rack is made so that the shelves do not meet at the center of the "V." There is a ½"- to 1"-wide gap between the two pieces of each trough shelf. This greatly simplifies the joinery because you can cut the tenons in a normal fashion. You don't need to do the inter-locking joint at the bottom of the trough, either, of course.

Bookshelf with "D" handles and keyed through tenon. Artist: Clarence Albers Zuppann. Collection of Terry and Jan Bender. Photo: Jan Bender

V

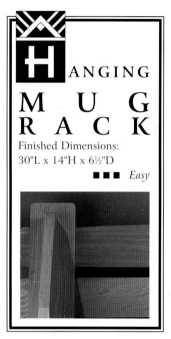

HANGING MUG RACK

Finished Dimensions:
30"L x 14"H x 6½"D

■ ■ ■ *Easy*

This is an attractive piece to hang on the wall for displaying items such as china, pottery, or metalwork. Although simple to build, it boasts through tenons, an arch at the bottom, and a pointed top. The difference in thickness between the back stretchers and the stiles also adds visual interest. If you add a plate groove to the shelf, this versatile rack can be used in any room of the house.

■ Required Techniques

Cutting a dado
Cutting a lap joint
Cutting a through tenon
Cutting a mortise

■ Cut List

2	Wide back stretchers	30" x 3½" x ¾"
1	Narrow back stretcher	30" x 2¾" x ¾"
2	Back stiles	14" x 3¼" x 1"
2	Sides	11½" x 5½" x ⅞"
1	Shelf	27¼" x 5" x ¾"

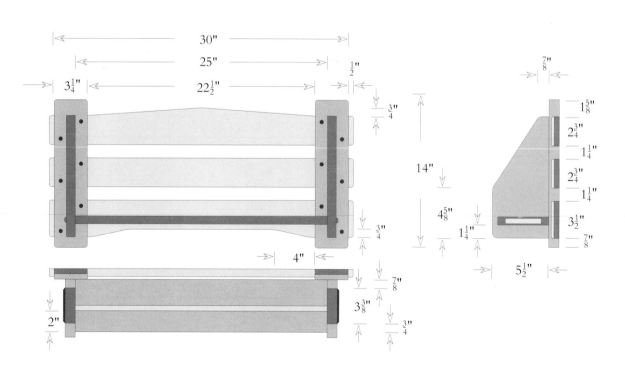

• I N S T R U C T I O N S •

1

Cut, plane, and square all stock.

BUILDING
THE BACK ASSEMBLY

2

Mark and cut lap joints ½" deep on the back stiles and back stretchers. Use a dado or a saw blade. Cut by making repeated passes with the blade. Alternatively, you may make a pair of saw cuts on the outside and remove the waste with a chisel. (See also the use of lap joints in the project instructions for the large, round tabouret, page 56).

3

Test for fit. NOTE: At this point, the top stretcher should be too wide to fit into its slot.

4

Cut the angle on the top stretcher where it comes to a point at the top. The narrow ends should fit into the lap joints cut on the stiles.

5

Draw and cut the decorative arch on the bottom stretcher.

6

Test fit all the parts you have cut to this point.

7

Round or chamfer the corners on all these parts.

8

Sand all cut parts.

9

Glue and clamp together the stretchers and stiles.

10

Use a pair of dowels to pin the stretchers to the stiles. See the information on doweling joints on page 36.

BUILDING THE SHELF ASSEMBLY

11

Cut the mortises in the sides for the shelf.

12

Cut the sides to shape and round the corners.

13

Cut the tenons of the shelf ends to fit into the mortises on the sides.

14

Cut the decorative chamfer on the ends of the tenons.

15

If desired, you may cut a plate groove in the shelf, 2" from the front edge, being careful not to cut into the tenons.

16

Sand the sides and the shelf.

17

Glue and clamp together.

18

After the glue has dried, clean up any excess glue.

ATTACHING THE BACK AND SHELF ASSEMBLIES

19

Place the back assembly face up on the bench and position and mark where the sides will fit onto the back stiles.

20

In the center of the area where the sides will sit, drill 3 screw holes from the front through each back stile and each back stretcher.

21

Countersink the screw holes from the back.

22

Glue and screw the side and shelf assembly to the back assembly.

23

After the glue dries, clean up any excess glue.

24

Plug the screw holes with dowels.

25

Do a final sanding. Your piece is now ready to finish.

In *The Craftsman*, this shelf was pictured hanging from a pair of chains. If you want to hang it from a picture rail with chains, drill a hole in the top of each back stile for hooks. Otherwise, you may attach a sturdy hanger on the back of each back stile and hang the shelf from 2 screws set into the wall. DO NOT USE PICTURE FRAME WIRE. You don't want the shelf to tip and dump the contents.

C LASSIC
ARCHED
FOOT-
STOOL

Finished Dimensions:
15"H x 16"W x 20"D

■ ■ ■ *Medium*

This arched footstool and its variation (page 91) appeared in an early article on manual training in *The Craftsman*. No measured drawing was provided so I have created a drawing and specifications here. Gustav Stickley considered this footstool and its variant to be of pure and simple design "fitted to be placed before the eyes of children and amateur craftsmen. They incorporate no vagaries of design and plainly express conceptions of rest and convenience."

This stool was sold as #300 in Gus Stickley's catalog. The variation without the arch was also identified as #300 in different catalogs, and would be a simpler project, as it would avoid cutting the curves.

I recommend building one of the stools before beginning a Morris chair. Not only does a footstool make a useful companion piece, but it will also serve as good practice on mortise and tenon joinery before undertaking the more demanding chair. If you build both pieces and plan to fume them, fume and finish the stool at the same time you do the chair for a better color match.

To upholster one of these stools, canvas should be stretched over the top rails and tacked on the inside. Webbing should be woven over the canvas and also tacked on the inside. A thin layer of stuffing or foam is laid on top of the webbing, and a layer of muslin is stretched over the rails and tacked in place. The upholstery fabric or leather then is stretched over the muslin and tacked into place. Decorative tacks are added next to the posts. Traditionally, sometimes a row of tacks was added along the arches as well.

■ **Required Techniques**

Cutting a through mortise
Cutting a blind mortise
Cutting through and blind tenons
Laying out and cutting curves

■ **Cut List**

4	Posts	15" x 1¼" x 1¼"
2	Long top rails	20½" x 4¼" x ¾"
2	Short top rails	16½" x 4¼" x ¾"
2	Long bottom rails	20½" x 1¼" x ¾"
2	Short bottom rails	16½" x 1¼" x ¾"

■ **Hardware and Supplies**

Upholstery materials
Decorative tacks

1

Cut, plane, and square all stock.

2

Mark the legs for mortises: decide which faces of the posts you like best and orient them the way you like them before cutting. NOTE: Because the top mortises are blind and the lower rails are of two different heights, diagonal pairs of legs are identical and adjacent legs are different! Study the drawing of the stool legs (figure 1).

3

Cut mortises, but do not cut blind mortises deeper than 1".

4

Cut tenons on all the rails. If you are not using hand tools, the tenons on the upper rails should be left the same length as the lower ones to ensure that the distance between the tenons is the same.

5

Miter the tenons on the upper rails and test fit the parts together.

6

Mark the curves for the upper rails and cut them. Leather or cloth will be wrapped around the edges of these rails, so round them with a router bit or sandpaper (photo 1).

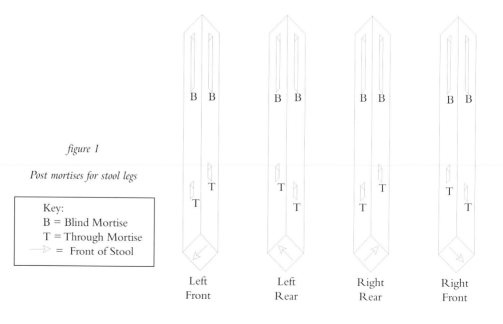

photo 1

Slate etchings, Grove Park Inn, Asheville, North Carolina

figure 1

Post mortises for stool legs

Key:
B = Blind Mortise
T = Through Mortise
⟶ = Front of Stool

Left
Front

Left
Rear

Right
Rear

Right
Front

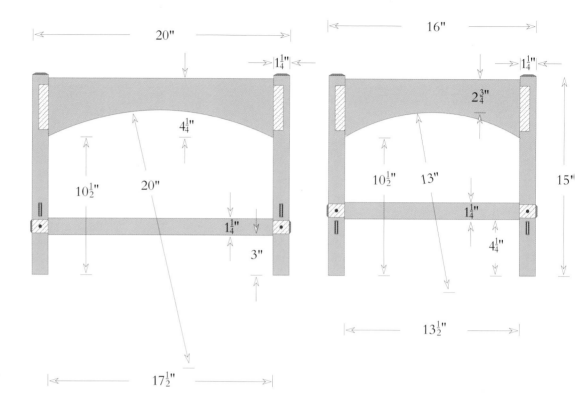

7

Chamfer the through tenons, the tops (and maybe the bottoms) of the posts.

8

Sand all the pieces, taking the "knife edge" off of them.

9

Decide how you want to orient the lower rails—you can mark them on the tenons.

10

Glue up each end of the stool, checking for squareness.

11

Pin the joints on the lower rail ends, then trim and sand them flush. (The upper rails are not pinned.)

12

Glue the ends to the long rails, checking for squareness.

13

Pin the remaining lower rail joints, trim, and sand flush.

14

Clean up all the glue. Do a final sanding. The piece is ready to finish.

15

Finish the footstool, remembering to clean it with a tack cloth first.

This footstool is easier to construct than the arched footstool (page 87) because there are no curves to lay out and cut. It also features easier-to-cut blind mortise and tenon joints.

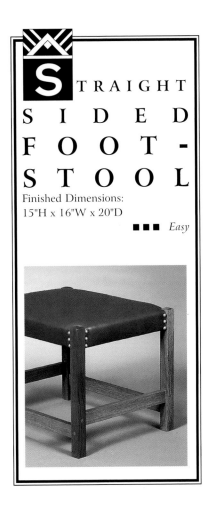

STRAIGHT SIDED FOOTSTOOL

Finished Dimensions:
15"H x 16"W x 20"D

■ ■ ■ *Easy*

■ Required Techniques

Cutting blind mortise and tenons

■ Cut List

4	Posts	15" x 1¼" x 1¼"
2	Long top rails	20½" x 2" x ¾"
2	Short top rails	16½" x 2" x ¾"
2	Long bottom rails	20½" x 1¼" x ¾"
2	Short bottom rails	16½" x 1¼" x ¾"

■ Hardware and Supplies

Upholstery materials
Decorative tacks

■ INSTRUCTIONS ■

1

Cut, plane, and square all stock.

2

Mark the legs for mortises: decide which faces of the posts you like best and orient them the way you like before cutting. NOTE: Because the lower rails are of two different heights, diagonal pairs of legs are identical and adjacent legs are different! Note the drawing of the stool legs (figure 1, page 92).

3

Cut mortises, but do not cut blind mortises deeper than 1".

4

Cut tenons on all the rails. If you are not using hand tools, the tenons on the upper rails should be left the same length as the lower ones to ensure that the distance between the tenons is the same.

5

Miter the tenons on the upper rails, and test fit the parts together.

6

To complete, follow steps 7-15 for the Arched Footstool on page 90.

20"

1¼"

2"

12¾"

3"

1¼"

16"

1¼"

2"

12¾"

1¼"

4¼"

13½"

Key:
B = Blind Mortise
T = Through Mortise
→ = Front of Stool

figure 1

Post mortises for stool legs

B B   B B   B B   B B

B   B   B   B
B   B   B   B

Left
Front

Left
Rear

Right
Rear

Right
Front

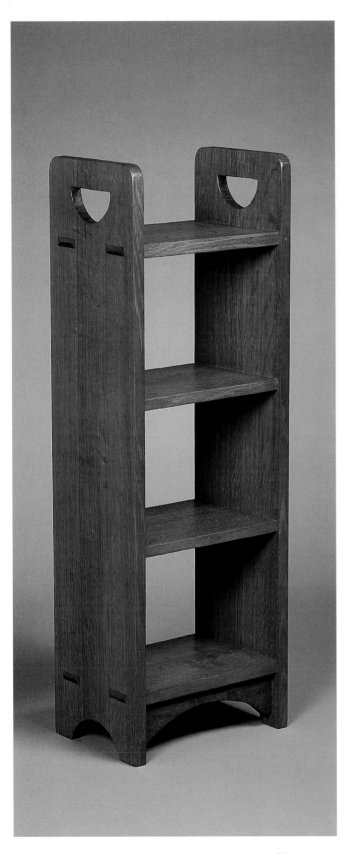

Finished Dimensions:
40"H x 14"W x 10"D

■ ■ ■ *Medium to Difficult*

This is another design that appeared in *The Craftsman*. Although the shelves are narrow, the stand is surprisingly handy and will create order from the mess that accumulates on your coffee table! It fits all of my woodworking magazines just fine. It's also great for books or for showing off art pottery. You can put a lamp or potted plant on the top shelf.

This library is a true period treasure. Old West End National Register Historic District, Toledo, Ohio.

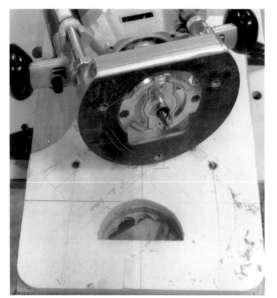

▪ *Required Techniques*

Cutting a through mortise

Cutting through tenons

Cutting a cutout

Biscuiting a joint

Doweling joints

▪ *Cut List*

2	*Sides*	*40" x 10" x 1"*
2	*Top & bottom shelves*	*15" x 9½" x 1"*
2	*Middle shelves*	*15" x 9½" x ¾"*
2	*Bottom braces*	*15" x 3" x 1"*

▪ I N S T R U C T I O N S ▪

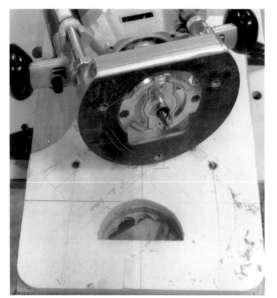

photo 1

1

Cut, plane, and square all stock. If you don't have wide enough boards for sides and shelves, glue them up. Use biscuits or dowels when you join your boards, or spline them. If you plan to use dowels, use a doweling jig to avoid alignment problems.

2

Before you cut the mortises, make the D-shaped holes and bottom cutouts. A turn-of-the-century home woodworker would have bored a hole, then used a coping saw to cut out the "D" shapes. You can do them that way, or use a hand-held saber saw, cleaning up the curves with wood rasps, files, and sandpaper. Another approach is to make a template of the "D" shape, and attach it to the side with screws where the mortise will eventually be cut. Using a sleeve on your router, make a series of light cuts until the shape is cut through (photo 1). Then clean up the sides with files or sandpaper.

3

Cut the through mortises for the top and bottom shelves. Cut long blind mortises for the two middle shelves (photo 2).

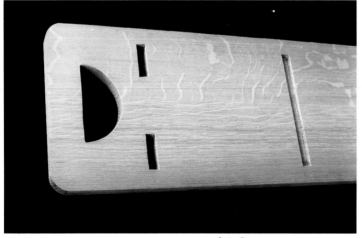

photo 2

4

Cut the tenons on the ends of the shelves. For through tenons, note that the spacing is critical for the twin tenons to line up properly with the mortises.

5

Check the fit of the tenons and trim as needed.

6

Bevel the ends of the through tenons.

7

Do your preliminary sanding, test clamp the sides to the shelves, then do your final glue up.

8

Pin the top and bottom shelves with dowels, and do a final sanding. Your stand is now ready to finish. Remember to sign your work after you apply finish.

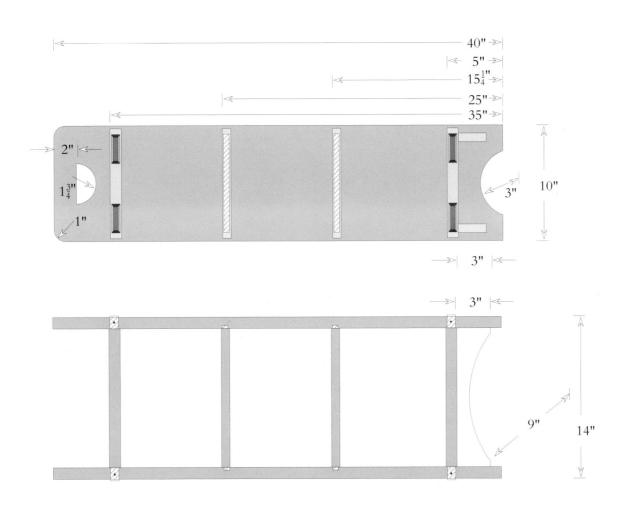

This charming period room features the original built-in window seat.

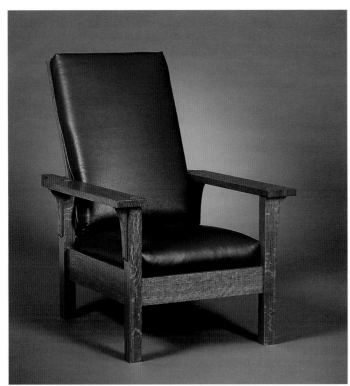

THE OPEN FLAT-ARM

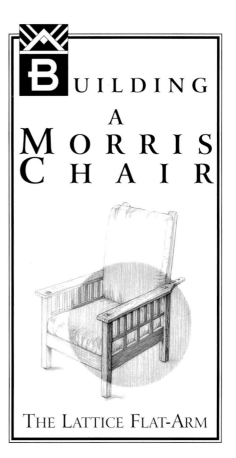

BUILDING A MORRIS CHAIR

THE LATTICE FLAT-ARM

THE SPINDLE FLAT-ARM

THE SLATTED FLAT-ARM

The following instructions describe the main procedures for building three Morris chairs—Open-Frame, Spindle, and Slatted Flat-Arm. The Lattice Flat-Arm starts out with several of the same steps, but then requires many different instructions to complete the chair. Read through the general instructions first, then read the specific instructions for the chair you want to build. Then you'll be ready to return to the general instructions and begin to make your chair.

▪ INSTRUCTIONS ▪

1

Cut, plane, and square all stock.

LEG POSTS

2

Cut, plane, and square all the stock. Glue each leg post out of two pieces of wood. You may want to use small wire nails as cleats to prevent the halves from moving. Pound two or three nails into one of the pieces, avoiding areas where you will be cutting or mortising later. Cut off the nails so that $1/16$" projects from the board. Press the boards together so that the projecting nails indent the facing board—this will prevent the boards from slipping out of alignment when they are clamped. Glue the two halves together.

3

After the glue is dry, trim the glued edges so they are flat and at right angles to the faces. The combined thickness of the glued stock should now be $2\frac{1}{4}$" x 2" wide. Trimming can be done on a table saw, jointer, or by hand with a long-bodied plane. Glue two pieces of $3/16$" veneer to the sides that show the glue seams. Trim and sand square so the edges of the veneer are even with the glued stock, yielding $2\frac{1}{4}$" x $2\frac{1}{4}$" posts.

MAKING VENEER FOR LEG STOCK

4

To obtain a $3/16$"-thick veneer: Use a band saw and fence to slice the boards vertically, or use a table saw to cut grooves to within $1/8$" of the center of the board. (Use feather boards and other safety devices.) Then, cut apart with a handsaw. Plane the veneer flat. You can also just plane the boards to $3/16$" thickness.

MORTISING THE ARMS

5

Determine the placement of the wood for armrests (this is important for chair aesthetics).

6

Mark and cut mortises in the chair arms. Clean out the mortises.

PYRAMIDAL TENONS

7

Cut the shoulders of the tenons on top of the posts. Cut the shoulders $1/8$" deeper than the final size of the tenon. Cut the faces of the tenons. Complete cutting the tenon on one post, then test fit it. Trim the end of each tenon from all 4 sides at a slight angle (10-12 degrees) to get a pyramid shape.

photo 2: The tenon shoulders are cut slightly deeper than the tenon.

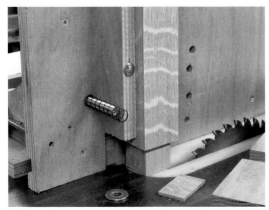

photo 3: Cutting tenon faces with a homemade jig

Leave each tenon a tiny bit oversized for fine tuning (photos 1-4).

8

Test the tenons on top of the leg posts for fit with the mortises above. Trim accordingly. Do all 4 posts, testing for fit as you

photo 4: Cutting decorative tops on leg tenons

work. Orient the posts so that the veneered face is forward. Position the mortises in the posts. Test fit the posts into the arms.

9

Mark the locations of all the mortises in the posts. To help check for correct placement, stand the posts on end, orienting them so that the veneered face is forward. The shorter back-rail mortises should face each other. Cut all the mortises in the posts.

HORIZONTAL RAILS

10

Position the lower rail under the arm, centered. Mark where the shoulders of the tenons will rest (photo 5, page 100).

11

Cut the tenon shoulders on the side rails, and the front and back rails.

12

Cut the faces for the tenons. Then, cut the tenons to width so that they fit into the mortises.

13

Test fit the rails into the posts. By gradually hand-fitting your chair, instead of completely cutting out all the parts ahead of time, you allow for any vagaries in your

photo 5: Marking the lower rail

18

Disassemble the chair and trim off a portion of each leg falling below the angle. Trimming the bottoms of the legs allows the seat to slope back for more comfort. This also improves the line of the chair, making it more sleek.

photo 6

own construction method as well as keep your chair square.

SHAPING THE ARMS

14

Cut the angle at the back of each arm. Because it's easier to measure and mortise the arms as square boards, now is the best time to cut the decorative angle.

15

Sand the arms.

TRIMMING THE BOTTOMS OF THE LEGS

16

Assemble but do not glue up the chair.

17

Working on one side of the chair, use a straight edge held from the floor at the front of the chair to about 1½" up the leg at the back. Draw a line on the post corresponding to the angle (photo 6).

photo 7

PREPARATION AND ASSEMBLY OF THE BASE

19

Fit together the chair frame. Look for any areas that need adjustment.

20

Sand surfaces smooth on all of the parts you have made to this point. You will need to sand later as well, but it's easy to sand what is not yet glued up.

GLUING UP THE BASE OF THE CHAIR

21

Lay out the parts prior to gluing up. Glue the lower rails to the posts.

22

Glue the slats or the spindles to the lower rail, if applicable to the design you are building.

photo 8: Turning the adjustment pegs; see step 40, page 102.

23

Glue the arm to the assembly and clamp. You may need additional clamps at the center of the arms to help clamp the slats or spindles (photo 7).

24

Glue up the other side of the chair in the same way.

25

Pin the mortises on the side assemblies. For instructions on pinning joints, see page 36. Glue up the other side. Pin the side joints with ⅜" dowels on the front, back, and arms. Glue the side assemblies to the front and back. Cut and sand the dowels flush.

26

Glue the side assemblies to the front and back rails, and pin.

BACKREST

27

Mark the location of the holes for the pivot pins, and drill holes ⅝" in diameter or ½" in diameter for the Lattice Flat-Arm Morris Chair.

28

Mark and cut the mortises for the slats.

29

Round off the top of the back posts for the lattice chair, or chamfer the post top for the other chairs.

30

Measure the distance between the arms on the chair frame and allow about ¼" on each side for clearance. Determine the width between the posts. Cut the slats to this length plus 2" (for tenons).

31

Cut the tenons on the ends of the slats.

32

Do preliminary sanding on slats and posts.

33

Glue the slats to one post, then glue the other side. Clamp.

34

Pin the mortises from the front.

ADDING CORBELS

35

Cut out the corbels.

36

Clamp them together and sand them as a unit. This will help to ensure a good fit at glue-up time. Check them for fit on your chair, trimming as necessary.

37

Glue the corbels to the posts.

38

Pin them with the dowels after the glue has dried.

BACK ADJUSTMENT MECHANISM

39

Mark the location for the two adjustment pins and cut them as described in step 40.

MAKING PIVOT PINS AND ADJUSTMENT PINS

40

After the base and the backrest are made, make the pivot and adjustment pins (figures 1 and 2). The lathe is rarely used for making Arts and Crafts style furniture (photo 8, page 101). If you don't own a lathe, have someone who does turning make pivot and adjustment pins for you. Drill test holes in a sample board so you can check the shaft diameter of the pins for fit. A small vertical lathe attachment for a drill press can also be used.

MAKING WOOD WASHERS

41

With the backrest centered between the back posts, measure how thick you want your washers to be. Glue up 2 pieces of wood face to face, with the grain at right angles. From this stock, you will want to cut at least 2 washers, 1" in diameter, though I would recommend making at least 4, in case you lose one later! (They make great cat toys.)

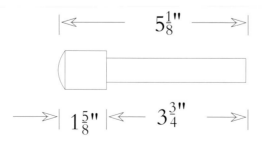

figure 1: Pivot pin

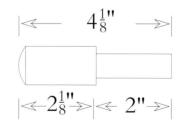

figure 2: Adjustment pin

42

Mark the centers of the holes and mark 1"- or 1¼"-diameter circles around these centers. Drill ⅝" holes in these centers, then cut the circles out, and round the outsides. You can complete the rounding by mounting the wood washer between a ⅝" bolt and nut, and chucking it in a drill press or lathe. Use lathe tools or sandpaper to even up the washers, and round the sharp edges slightly.

43

Check the fit on the pivot pins. The purpose of the washers is to keep the back of the chair from scraping the arms. The washers should be thick enough to do the job, but allow ⅛" for expansion of wood due to humidity.

MAKING A SUPPORT TO HOLD AN UPHOLSTERED SEAT

44

Cut out and sand the cleats. About ¾" down from the top of the front and back rails, screw on the cleats, with at least 5 screws per cleat. Predrill and countersink the holes. If you do not provide your upholsterer with a seat frame (photo 9), you could end up with a piece of plywood for the base of your seat.

You can make a haunched mortise and tenon seat frame and pin the joints. You will want to allow at least ⅛" clearance all the way around it to allow for the use of webbing and other upholstery materials.

For upholstery advice, see page 38.

PLACING PIVOT HOLES IN THE CHAIR BASE

45

After the base and backrest are glued up, set the backrest between the arms—you want

photo 9

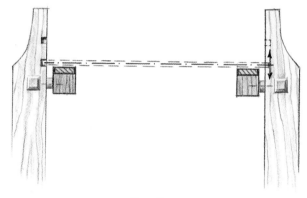

figure 3

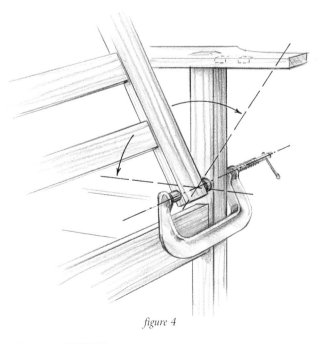

figure 4

the backrest to be sitting over the front and back rails. Make a pair of blocks to keep the back centered between the front legs. Set a block between each arm and the backrest. Prop up the backrest, while keeping it centered between the back posts, so that the pivot holes on the backrest are positioned as shown in figures 3 and 4 on page 103.

46

Cut a pair of ⅝" dowels to fit through the holes in the backrest. Push them through the holes, keeping everything aligned. Clamp the dowels so they are centered against the posts. Lift the top of the backrest. Make sure that it doesn't hit the arms and that it is centered. Move the backrest upright. If the backrest hits any part of the chair base, adjust your clamping. There should be a ½" gap between the backrest and the post on each side of the chair.

47

Take a pencil and trace the circumference of the dowel onto each back post. Mark (dent) the center of your circle with an awl or nail. Use a stop collar on the drill to avoid drilling all the way through the post. Insert the pivot pins. Now you can swing the backrest. (If you have a fit problem and you need to re-drill the hole, you can cover up

your mistake by using a dowel to fill it in. Glue it in, cut it off, and sand flush. Start over with your pivot hole.)

48

Once your pivot holes are done, put the wood washers on the pins between the backrest and the posts. If the fit is too tight, you may need to sand the washers to make them thinner. Washers are just spacers, so the backrest should still swing freely.

PLACING ADJUSTMENT HOLES ON THE INSIDE BACK OF THE CHAIR ARMS

49

You can use a pencil to mark the centers of the holes for the adjustment pins; mark all 4 holes on each side of the chair (figure 5). Swing the backrest along the arc to the hole position. Check each position. Make sure that the backrest lines up at each position. You can position yourself behind the chair and pull the backrest toward you. Using 2 nails as guides, hold them against each armrest where the opposite adjustment holes should be. You should hold the nails so that they are also against the backrest, using them as pointers. Adjust as necessary. Mark the correct position with an awl, then drill.

50

At this point, all of your chair parts should be ready for assembly. The easiest way to assemble your chair is to set the backrest between the arms (over the front and back rails again). Now you can install the pins and washers. Once the frame of the chair is assembled, you may add a drop-in seat and a loose back cushion.

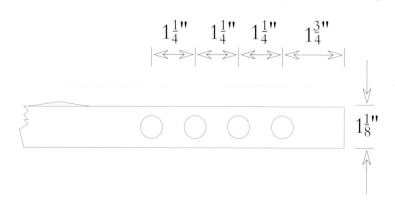

figure 5: Adjustment pin spacing

This design is the easiest of my Morris chair series. It has very simple lines but fulfills its purpose as a recliner quite well. Its wide side boards can display figured wood beautifully.

O P E N
F R A M E
FLAT-ARM
M O R R I S
C H A I R

Finished Dimensions:
37"D x 43"H x 30½"W

■ ■ ■ *Medium to Difficult*

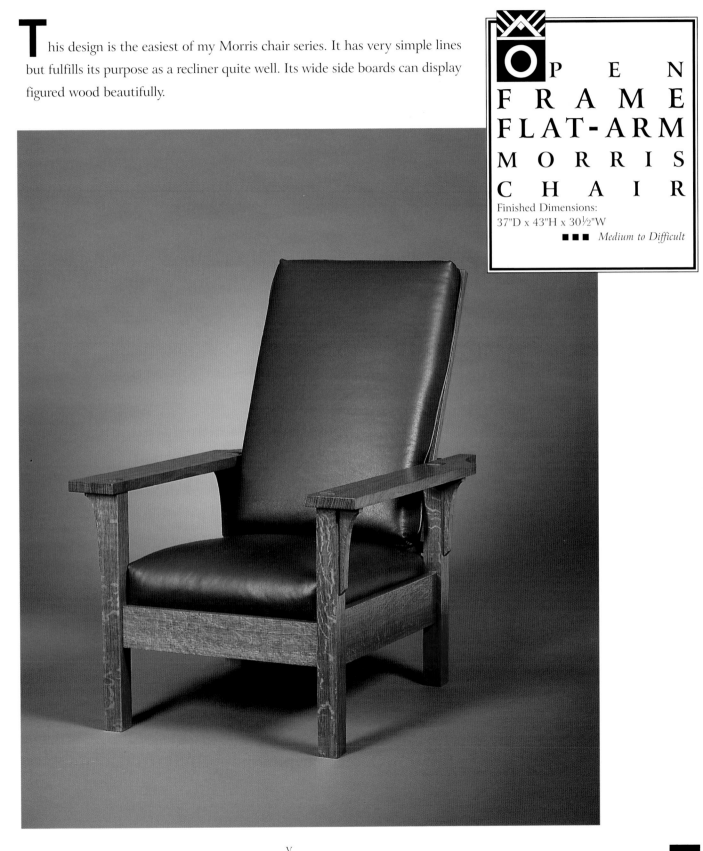

▪ Required Techniques

Cutting a through mortise
Cutting a blind mortise
Cutting through and blind tenons
Making leg posts
Making pivot pins
Making wood washers

▪ Cut List

BASE

8	Leg halves	24" x 2¼" x 1¼" ⁺⁺
8	Leg veneers	24" x 2¼" x ¼"** ⁺⁺
2	Arms	37" x 5" x ⅞"
2	Side rails	26" x 3" x ⅞"
1	Front rail	26" x 4" x ⅞"
1	Back rail	26" x 3" x ⅞"
4	Corbels	8" x 2" x 1"

⁺⁺ allow extra width; they will be trimmed after posts are glued up

**probably resawn from thicker stock

BACK

2	Back posts	31" x 1¾" x ⅞"
4	Back slats	22" x 2¾" x 3/8"
2	Pivot pins	(see figure 1 on page 102)
2	Adjustment pins	(see figure 2 on page 102)

ADDITIONAL

2	Seat frame rails	24" x 2¾" x ⅞"
2	Seat frame stiles	24" x 2¾" x ⅞"
2	Cleats	18" x ⅞" x ⅞"
	Dowels	⅜"
2	Stock for wood washers	4" x 4" x ⅜"

▪ Hardware and Supplies

Screws for cleats
Upholstery materials

▪ INSTRUCTIONS ▪

A

Complete steps 1-13 on pages 98-100. See figure 1 for handling of post mortises.

B

Miter the ends of the tenons where they meet so that they don't interfere with each other (photo 1).

C

Complete steps 14-21 on pages 100-101.

D

SKIP step 22, then continue with steps 23-50 on pages 101-104.

photo 1: Blind mortises and mitered tenons

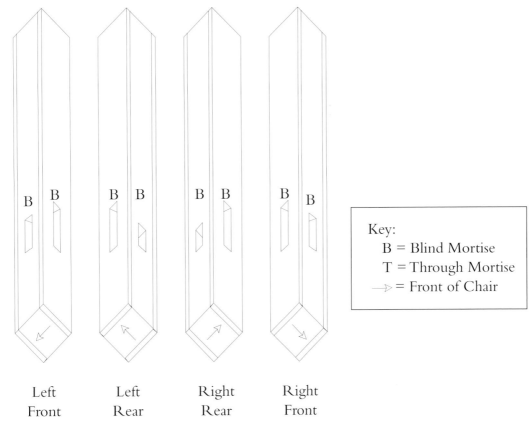

| Left Front | Left Rear | Right Rear | Right Front |

figure 1: Orientation of post mortises

V

OPEN FRAME FLAT-ARM MORRIS CHAIR

Open Frame Flat-Arm Morris Chair

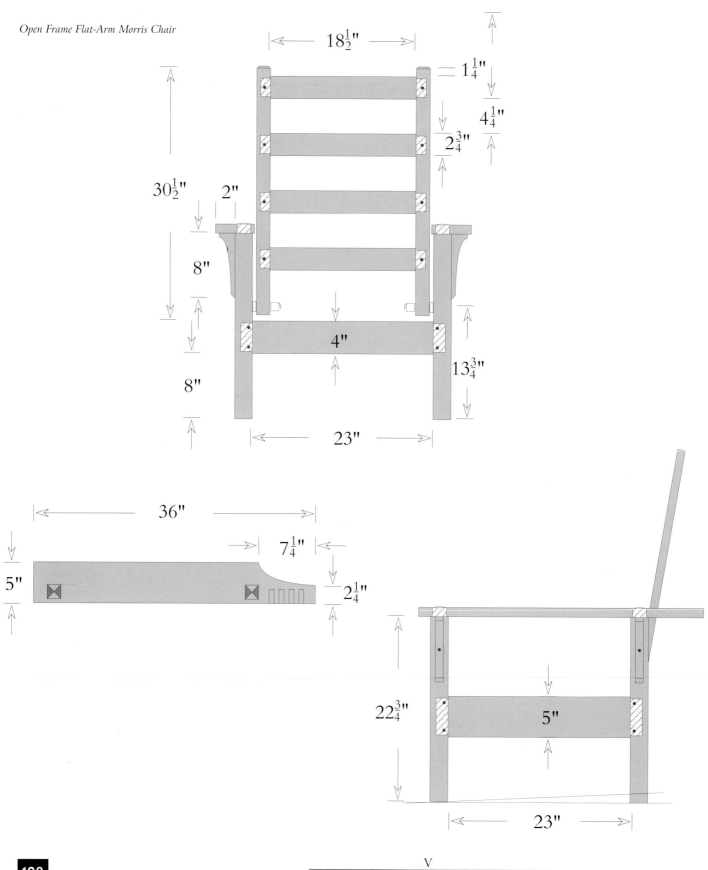

'm sentimental about this design; its side treatment resembles that of the Gus chair owned by my grandfather, August Kemner. Gus made a version with 5"-wide lower side rails, and the slats were 2" shorter on his chair.

SLATTED FLAT-ARM MORRIS CHAIR

Finished Dimensions:
37"D x 43"H x 30½"W

■ ■ ■ *Difficult*

▪ Required Techniques

Cutting a through mortise
Cutting a blind mortise
Cutting through and blind tenons
Making leg posts
Making pivot pins
Making wood washers

▪ Cut List

BASE

8	Leg halves	24" x 1¼" x 2¼" ++
8	Leg veneers	24" x 2¼" x ¼"** ++
10	Slats	19" x 3" x ⅜"
2	Arms	37" x 5" x 1⅛"
2	Side rails	28" x 3" x ⅞"
1	Front rail	28" x 4" x ⅞"
1	Back rail	28" x 4" x ⅞"
4	Corbels	8" x 2" x 1"

++ *allows extra width; they will be trimmed after posts are glued up*
** *probably resawn from thicker stock*

BACK

2	Back posts	31" x 1¾" x ⅞"
4	Back slats	22" x 2¾" x ⅜"
2	Pivot pins	(see figure 1 on page 102)
2	Adjustment pins	(see figure 2 on page 102)

ADDITIONAL

2	Seat frame rails	24" x 2¾" x ⅞"
2	Seat frame stiles	24" x 2¾" x ⅞"
2	Cleats	18" x ⅞" x ⅞"
	Dowels	⅜"
2	Stock for wood washers	4" x 4" x ⅜"

▪ Hardware and Supplies

Screws for cleats
Upholstery materials

▪ I N S T R U C T I O N S ▪

A

Complete steps 1-13 on pages 98-100. See figure 1 for handling of post mortises.

B

SLATS

Mark the lower rail for the evenly spaced slat mortises. Transfer these locations to the underside of the arm. Cut mortises for the slats. Fit the lower rail, front and back posts, and arm together. Mark the length of the slat between the tenon shoulders and cut the slat tenons. Do this on all of the slats.

C

Complete steps 14-50 on pages 100-104.

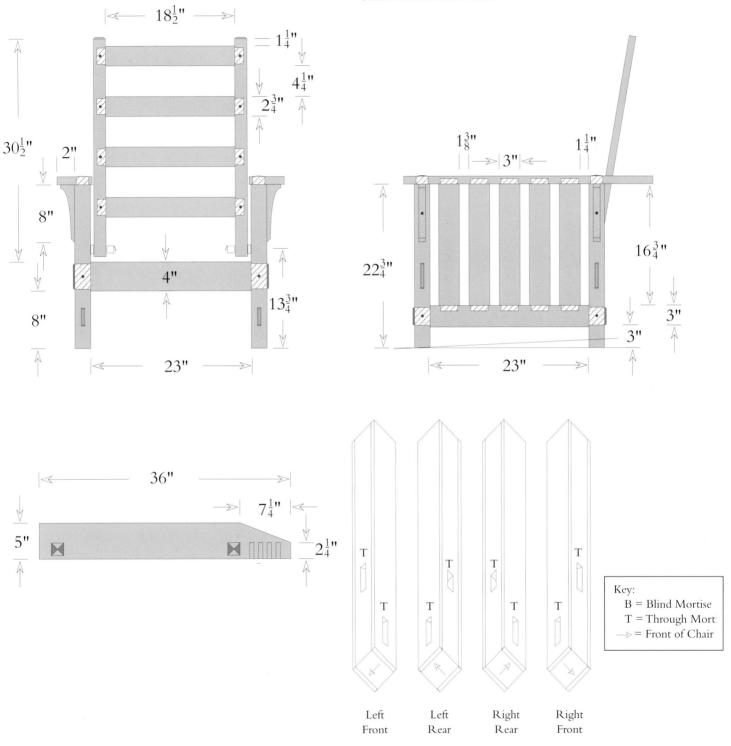

figure 1: Orientation of post mortises

Key:
B = Blind Mortise
T = Through Mort
⟶ = Front of Chair

Left
Front

Left
Rear

Right
Rear

Right
Front

V

BUILDING ARTS & CRAFTS FURNITURE

The spindle treatment is what many people call to mind when they think of the terms "Arts and Crafts" or "Mission." Certainly, this is an elegant and challenging design to build with its 60 mortise and tenon joints for the spindles alone. This is not a project for the faint of heart. It also features long corbels under the arms, through mortises on the posts, plus additional blind mortises. Antique spindle Morris chairs are rare because the extra labor made them more expensive.

SPINDLE
**F L A T -
A R M**
M O R R I S
C H A I R

Finished Dimensions:
37"D x 43"H x 30½"W

■ ■ ■ *Difficult*

■ **Required Techniques**

Cutting a through mortise
Cutting a blind mortise
Cutting through and blind tenons
Making leg posts
Making pivot pins
Making wood washers

■ **Cut List**

BASE

8	Leg halves	24" x 2¼" x 1¼"++
8	Leg veneers	24" x 2¼" x ¼"** ++
30	Spindles	19" x ¾" x ¾"
4	Corbels	11" x 2" x 1"
2	Arms	37" x 5" x 1⅛"
2	Side rails	29" x 3" x ⅞"
1	Front rail	27" x 4" x ⅞"
1	Back rail	27" x 3" x ⅞"

++ *allow extra width; they will be trimmed after posts are glued up*

** *probably resawn from thicker stock*

BACK

2	Back posts	31" x 1¾" x ⅞"
4	Back slats	22" x 2¾" x ⅜"
2	Pivot pins	(see figure 1 on page 102)
2	Adjustment pins	(see figure 2 on page 102)

ADDITIONAL

2	Seat frame rails	24" x 2¾" x ⅞"
2	Seat frame stiles	24" x 2¾" x ⅞"
2	Cleats	18" x ⅞" x ⅞"
	Dowels	⅜"
2	Stock for wood washers	4" x 4" x ⅜"

■ **Hardware and Supplies**

Screws for cleats
Upholstery materials

■ **I N S T R U C T I O N S** ■

A

Complete steps 1-13 on pages 98-100. See figure 1 on page 115 for handling of post mortises. NOTE: The front and back rails fit into the blind mortises.

B

SPINDLES

To save on material costs, some woodworkers building in quartersawn white oak will cut spindles from slab-sawn wood, orienting the spindles so that the quartersawn sides face outward. Because the slab-sawn wood is usually cut from a different tree, this can present problems. If you plan to use slab-sawn along with quartersawn wood and you also plan to fume your chair, fume test samples for color matching prior to fuming your chair (and preferably prior to making the spindles). If you see a large color variation from the fuming test, you may prefer to use quartersawn stock for your spindles so that they match the rest of the chair.

C

Mark the lower rail for the 15 evenly spaced spindle mortises. Transfer these locations to the underside of the arm. Cut ⅜" mortises. Fit the lower rail, front and

photo 1: Test–fitting spindles

photo 2: Test–fitting spindles

back posts, and arm together. Mark the length of the spindle between the tenon shoulders and cut the spindle tenons. Do this on all of the spindles (photos 1 and 2).

D

Complete steps 14-38 on pages 100-102. Note that these corbels are longer and have a different shape from the open and slat chairs. Complete steps 39-50 on pages 102-104.

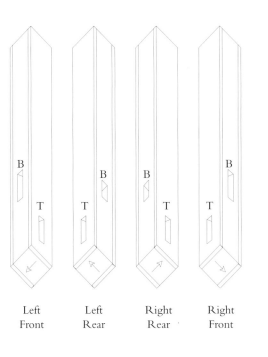

| Left Front | Left Rear | Right Rear | Right Front |

Key:
B = Blind Mortise
T = Through Mortise
——▷ = Front of Chair

figure 1: Orientation of post mortises

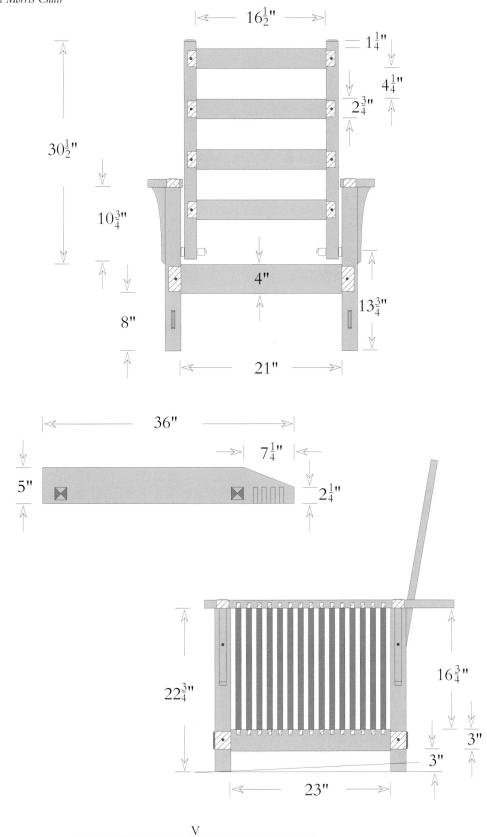

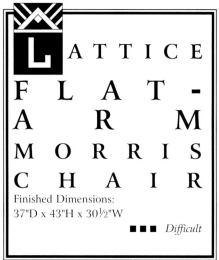

LATTICE FLAT-ARM MORRIS CHAIR

Finished Dimensions:
37"D x 43"H x 30½"W

■ ■ ■ *Difficult*

This unique variation on the Morris chair theme features an unusual side treatment. The design appeared in *The Craftsman*, and, although Gus Stickley never made the chair commercially, it's a good deal more sophisticated than the designs of many manufactured pieces made during the Arts and Crafts period. The designs of some of Gus's imitators were crude at times, bringing to mind the negative connotations of the word "rustic." Unlike the other reclining chairs included in this book, this one adjusts to three rather than four positions and does not use corbels.

In *The Craftsman*, the drawing, measurements, and cut list are inconsistent. I have corrected these problems in my version here.

■ Required Techniques

Cutting a through mortise
Cutting a blind mortise
Cutting through and blind tenons
Making leg posts
Making pivot pins
Making wood washers

■ Cut List

BASE

8	Leg halves	24" x 2¼" x 1¼" ++
8	Leg veneers	24" x 2¼" x ¼" ** ++
2	Arms	37" x 4½" x 1⅛"
2	Side rails	27" x 5" x 1¼"
1	Front rail	27" x 5" x 1¼"
1	Back rail	27" x 3" x 1¼"

++allow extra width; they will be trimmed
after posts are glued up
**probably resawn from thicker stock

ADDITIONAL SIDE PIECES

2	Horizontal side frets	25" x ¾" x 1¼"
10	Vertical side frets	6" x ¾" x 1¼"

BACK

2	Back posts	31" x 1¾" x 2"
4	Back slats	22" x 2¾" x ⅜"
2	Pivot pins	6" x 1¼" x 1¼"
1	Adjusting piece	27" x 1" x 1⅜"

ADDITIONAL

2	Seat frame rails	24" x 2¾" x 1"
2	Seat frame stiles	24" x 2¾" x 1"
1	Dowel	⅜"
2	Stock for wood washers	4" x 4" x ⅜"

■ Hardware and Supplies

Screws for cleats
Upholstery materials

■ INSTRUCTIONS ■

A

Complete steps 1-9 on pages 98-99. See figure 1 on page 120 for handling of post mortises.

B

HORIZONTAL RAILS

Position the lower rail under the arm, centered. Mark where the shoulders of the tenons will rest. Do the same with the fretwork rail. Cut the tenon shoulders on the side rails, horizontal fretwork, and front and back rails. Cut the faces for the tenons. Then cut the tenons to width. Test fit the rails into the posts. By gradually hand-fitting your chair, instead of completely cutting out all the parts ahead of time, you allow for any vagaries in your own construction method as well as keep your chair square.

C

VERTICAL FRETS

On the top of the horizontal fretwork rail, mark the mortises for the 7 evenly-spaced vertical frets. Transfer the mortise locations to the underside of the horizontal fretwork rail for the 3 vertical frets that go to the lower rail. Use the horizontal fretwork rail to transfer the 7 mortise locations to the under-

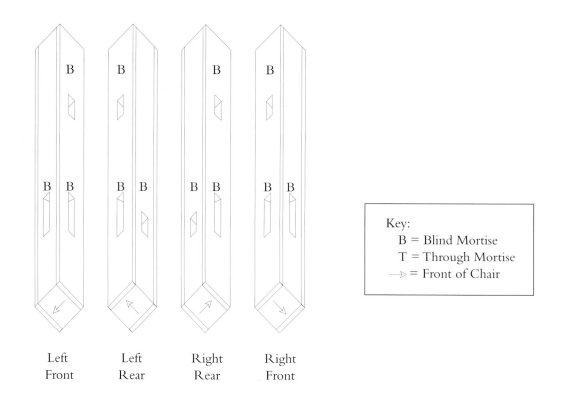

Key:
B = Blind Mortise
T = Through Mortise
⟶ = Front of Chair

Left
Front

Left
Rear

Right
Rear

Right
Front

figure 1: Orientation of post mortises

side of the arm. Also transfer the 3 mortise locations from the underside to the top of the lower rail. Cut the mortises for the vertical fretwork. On the vertical fretwork, mark the shoulder length, and cut the tenons, using the method from the horizontal rails.

D

Complete steps 14-19 on pages 100-101.

E

GLUING UP THE BASE OF THE CHAIR

Lay out the parts prior to gluing up. Glue the bottom rail to the 3 vertical frets, and glue the horizontal fret. Glue the post tenon to the leg post on the side assembly. Glue the tenons of the upper vertical frets into the horizontal fret. Put glue on the post tenons and on the upper fretwork

tenons. Fit the arm onto the posts and frets. Clamp. You may need additional clamps in the middle of the arms to clamp them to the frets. Glue up the other side of the chair the same way. Pin the mortises on the side assemblies. For instruction on pinning joints, see page 36. Glue the side assemblies to the front and back rails, and pin.

F

Complete steps 27-34 on pages 101-102.

G

BACK ADJUSTMENT MECHANISM

The original published plans for this chair used a bar with notches in the arms. You can use this method (described on page 121) or you can use 2 adjustment pins with holes as described in steps 39 & 40 on page 102.

Mark the location for the notches as described on page 102. Using a backsaw, make right-angle cuts that connect the outside edge and the bottom of the notches (figures 2 and 3). Use a chisel to remove the waste, taking light cuts (figure 4). Make the bar fit, allowing a little play to compensate for changes in humidity.

H

Complete steps 40-43 on pages 102-103. If you are using an adjustment bar, you will not need adjustment pins.

I

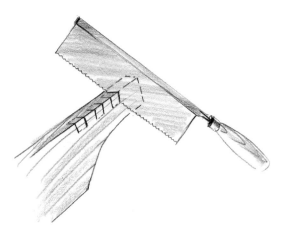

figure 2

MAKING A SUPPORT TO HOLD AN UPHOLSTERED SEAT

The original published design for this chair had supports on all 4 sides slanting toward the back rail. Holes are drilled about 1" apart, all around. Cane or cord was woven between these holes, and a seat pillow about 4" to 5" thick was placed on top. You can also use a frame seat with front and rear cleats, as shown in the other Morris chair directions in this book.

For seat-support information, follow step 44 on page 103.

J

Complete steps 45-50 on pages 103-104.

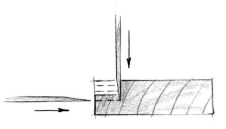

figure 3

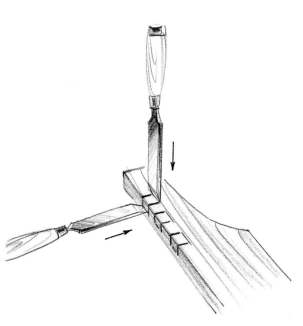

figure 4

V

LATTICE FLAT-ARM MORRIS CHAIR

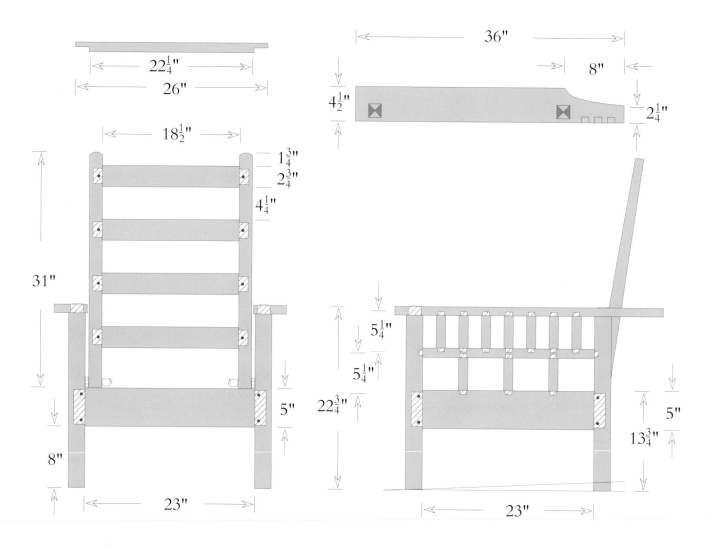

A Craftsman Cottage

Designed by Karl H. Nickel

THIS unusual and attractive little cottage, which was built some time ago in California, is intended to express the Craftsman idea in house-building.

Article in The Ladies' Home Journal, *1911*

ROUND **DINING** T A B L E

Finished Dimensions:
54" in diameter x 30"H
(extending to 9'11")

■ ■ ■ *Difficult*

This table is a very clean, simple design, the epitome of the Craftsman ideal in furniture. Its plans appeared in Gus's magazine, and he also manufactured the design for a number of years. Later versions had a slightly thinner top, 1" thick. It was made in a range of sizes: 48", 54", and 60" in diameter, and could extend from 8' to 12'.

If you change the width and number of the leaves, keep in mind the weight of the wood. A 16"-wide leaf is very heavy.

You might consider using casters on this piece due to its great weight, and to avoid damaging a floor or rug when moving it or taking leaves on or off. Furniture cups can be used under the casters to keep the table from rolling unintentionally.

■ ***Required Techniques***
Steam bending
Laying out and cutting curves

■ ***Cut List***
Enough lumber for a 54" round top, 1⅜" thick, plus:

5	Leaves	54" x 13" x 1⅜"
5	Leg posts	29" x 4" x 4"
4	Apron pieces	44" x 3½" x ¾"
8	Apron support blocks	8" x 3½" x 3"
10	Leaf aprons	13" x 3½" x 3/4"
4	Leg supports	18" x 3½" x 1"
1	Center leg support	22" (approx.) x 6" x ¾"

■ ***Hardware and Supplies***

2	Commercial table slides (wood)
5	Casters or heavy glides
12 pr.	Table alignment clips
	Table irons
	Assorted screws
	Table locks

■ I N S T R U C T I O N S ■

1

Cut, plane, and square all stock.

2

Select and position the wood for the tabletop.

3

Cut recesses for biscuits or splines, or drill holes for dowels.

4

Glue and clamp the two halves of the tabletop. DO NOT CUT THE CIRCLE YET.

5

Glue and clamp the leaves. When the glue is dry, plane and sand so that the top is flat and the joints are level.

6

For leg stock, use either 5 solid posts, or glue up boards for the 5 legs (taking care that when you eventually cut the tapers of the legs you do not cut into a glue seam).

7

Plane and square the legs so that all sides are at right angles to each other.

V

8

Cut the legs to final length so that all surfaces are flat and square to each other.

9

Decide which end of the leg will be the top. Mark it. (The top 4" of each leg is left square, and the taper starts below that.)

10

Mark where the tapers will be, and cut them roughly to shape on a band saw. You can also taper them on a jointer. Check the

tool's manual for safe operation. Clean the tapers on a jointer. Alternatively, you can use a long-bodied plane to clean them. NOTE: The legs are too big to cut the tapers on a table saw (photo 1).

11

Sand any planing or saw marks off the legs.

12

If you are using ball-bearing casters, drill holes in the bottoms of the legs so the casters will project about ¼". Use a Forstner bit

photo 1

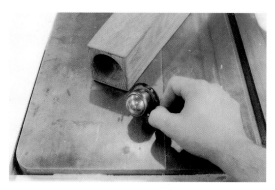

photo 2

and all, out of solid beams. That approach would have resulted in structurally weak table aprons—and that was not how he manufactured them.

13

After your ¾" stock for the aprons is cut to the approximate width and left overlength, steam bend it. See steam bending instructions for the dining/side chair on pages 69-70.

My 1"-thick oak did not bend easily to the correct radius; I was worried about breakage. I let the wood air dry for a day or so, and then resawed it into two ⅜"-thick boards (photo 3). They steam bent easily. After they were bent, clamped, and dried, I laminated them into four ¾" apron pieces.

photo 3

14

Mark the underside of the table with the radius of the top. Draw your circle using trammel points (available from a woodworking-product dealer) or a nail and pencil clamped to a piece of wood.

15

Draw a circle on the underside of the tabletop to mark the location of an apron.

16

From the center of the 2 circles, draw 2 lines at a 45-degree angle until they meet

sized for your caster to drill a flat-bottomed hole (photo 2). If you are not using casters, use heavy-duty glides that you can apply after finishing.

A P R O N S

Gus's plans for this piece in *The Craftsman* had the reader saw the apron pieces, curves the apron. This will be where each of the 4 outer legs will center. Mark these 4 locations by drawing a square for each. The legs will project about ½" beyond the apron.

17

Match the bent apron pieces to the circle you drew, as closely as possible. It is not absolutely vital that the aprons form a perfect radius, as long as they meet the legs at the right places. Mark where you will need to cut the aprons to meet the legs.

18

The side of each square representing the back of the leg (facing the center of the top) should be drawn as a continuous line until it intersects the apron line (figure 1). This line indicates the location of support blocks that should be attached to the inside of the apron. Mark the location of the support blocks on the underside of the tabletop.

19

Place the apron pieces against their markings on the underside of the top. Mark the aprons where they hit the legs. Trim the aprons so they are slightly over length. Cut 2 apron pieces in half at the line where the two halves of the table join.

MAKING TEMPLATES FOR CORNER BLOCKS

20

Because you may not have bent the apron pieces to a perfect radius, you will need to make each support block fit its own location. Using pieces of paper like carpenter squares, set them at the corners of each table leg and support block to the left and right of each leg along the apron, and tape them down. Then position the apron pieces on top of them.

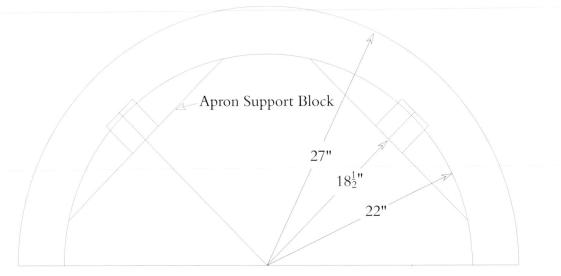

Apron Support Block

27"

18½"

22"

figure 1

21

Draw a line on the paper on the inside edge of each apron. Mark the tabletop, the paper, and the apron with a unique number so you can match up each part to its position.

22

For blocks: either cut stock or glue up scrap wood. Once blocks are cut (and glue has dried) square and plane them.

23

Cut out your patterns so that you have curved patterns to mark the blocks. Mark them and cut out the curves. Sand them to fit the aprons. Glue the blocks to the aprons. I used the waste cut from the blocks to help clamp the joints. I also used cutoff wire nails to keep the parts from sliding. (A similar use of wire nails is discussed in the instructions for a Morris chair, page 98.)

24

Sand the ends of the support blocks and aprons so they are flat and fit against the legs. (I used a disk sander.)

25

Cut a leg support that screws to the back of the leg and the support blocks on each side of the leg.

26

Drill and countersink holes to screw the leg supports to the legs (photo 4). Drill angled holes through the leg support into the support blocks. They angle away from the leg to help draw the support blocks against the leg. Then screw the parts together. Check for fit. Sand if adjustment is necessary.

27

Drill shallow holes into the apron for table irons. You may also drill counter-bored

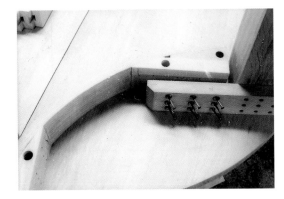

photo 4

holes through the support blocks for screws (similar to figure 1 on page 60).

28

Screw the apron and leg assembly to the bottom of the tabletop. Be careful that you are using the correct length screws so that they do not pass through the top.

29

Disassemble the parts.

TOP

30

Cut the curve of the tabletop using a band saw, saber saw, or bow saw. Even it up with a router and trammel attachment, if you wish. Sand the edge smooth. Make sure that the 2 halves are the same size and match up.

LEAVES

31

Cut leaves to match the diameter of the top. Mark where the apron for the leaves will go. Sand.

32

Cut the leaf aprons to length and sand.

33

Attach with table irons (photo 5, 128).

photo 5

TABLE ASSEMBLY

34

Place the 2 halves of the top together upside down on a workbench or a padded floor. Attach the aprons and the 4 outer legs. Position the table slides so they are at right angles to the split in the top. I cut an angle on the outside corners of the slides so they could be mounted farther apart (photo 6).

photo 6

35

Cut a center leg support. Sand it. Drill and countersink 3 holes on each end of the support so it can be screwed to the center board of each table slide. Screw it down.

36

Leaving your assembly upside down, place the center leg upside down against the support board. Mark where it hits the board.

Trim the center leg to length and sand, if desired. Then position the center leg on top of the support board diagonal to the board. Mark around the outside of the leg on the board.

37

Take the center board off the table slides. Drill and countersink holes through the support board and screw the leg to it. Remember to drill pilot holes into the leg first. Reattach the support board to the table slides. Flip the table over (get some strong helpers!). If the table is too heavy to move all at once, unscrew the table slides from half of the table and set the half with the center leg upright. Turn the other half over and position it on top of the table slides attached to the half with the center leg. Make sure the halves are aligned.

photo 7: Table alignment clips

Attach the table alignment clips and be sure they are centered and set at the same distance from the edge of the table.

38

Pull the halves of the table apart. Put 1 leaf in and attach the alignment clips so they match up with the ones on the table. Repeat this step for any remaining leaves. Put all the leaves into the table. Check for fit. Disassemble and sand as necessary.

39

Do a final sanding of table. You are now ready to finish. Remove all hardware. I recommend finishing this project in pieces.

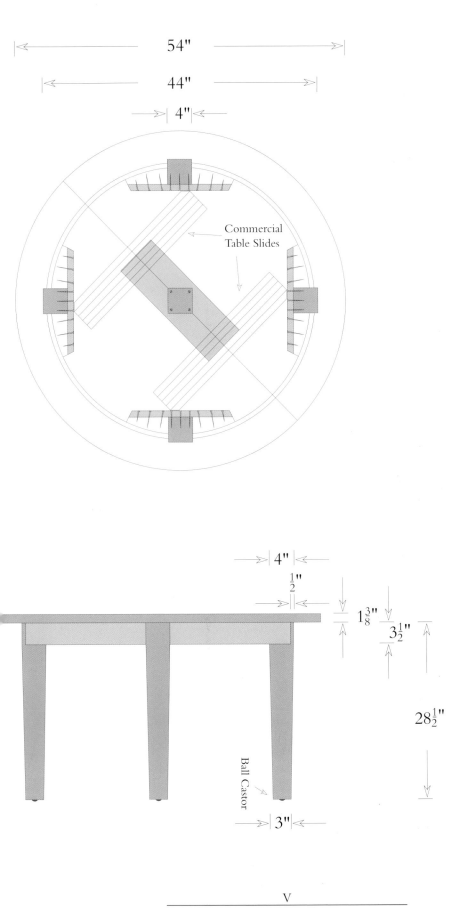

54"

44"

4"

Commercial
Table Slides

4"

$\frac{1}{2}$

$1\frac{3}{8}$"

$3\frac{1}{2}$"

$28\frac{1}{2}$"

Ball Castor

3"

The Ladies' Home Journal *advertisement,*
1907

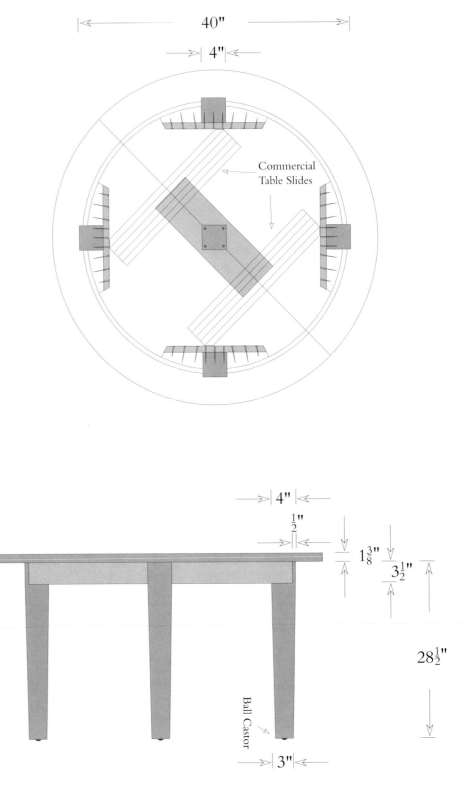

48"

40"

4"

Commercial
Table Slides

4"

$\frac{1}{2}$"

$1\frac{3}{8}$"

$3\frac{1}{2}$"

$28\frac{1}{2}$"

Ball Castor

3"

The Ladies' Home Journal
advertisement, 1913

This 1908 brick four-square home, located in the Old West End National Register Historic District in Toledo, Ohio, features the original woodwork and fireplace.

V

ROUND DINING TABLE

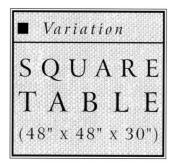

This simpler square dining table design can meet household needs nicely, and can actually seat more people than a round table of the same size. Not only does this version avoid the labor of steam bending, but also the extra work of cutting the round top. Choice of table shapes is often a purely aesthetic decision, however.

This is a big, beautiful glass-door bookcase with through tenons on the sides, arches, and period style hardware. I used new hand-hammered round copper pulls that look like the originals. The bookcase was illustrated in *The Craftsman* magazine, and also sold through Gus Stickley's catalog. It will hold a substantial number of books, and also pottery and other collectibles, particularly on the top. Its projecting back and sides add some protection for these items.

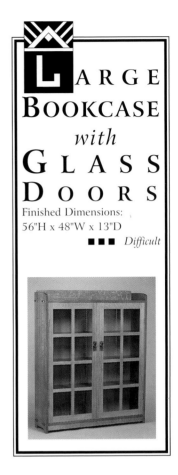

LARGE BOOKCASE *with* GLASS DOORS

Finished Dimensions:
56"H x 48"W x 13"D
■ ■ ■ *Difficult*

■ Required Techniques
Cutting a through mortise
Cutting a through tenon
Cutting curves
Splining boards

■ Cut List
Case

2	Sides	56" x 13" x 1⅛"
2	Top & bottom	50" x 12¼" x 1⅛"
3	Middle shelves	49" x 10½" x ¾"
1	Bottom front	49" x 2¼" x 1"
1	Bottom back	49" x 2¾" x 1"
1	Center post	49" x 1¾" x 1⅜"
2	Hinge supports	49" x 1" x ⅜"

Back boards, 6 to 15 boards of equal width will be required to create a chamfer and spline back 50"H x 47"W

■ Doors

4	Verticals (frame rails)	48" x 2" x 1"
4	Horizontals (frame stiles)	22" x 2½" x 1"
2	Vertical mullions	48" x 1¼" x 1"
6	Horizontal mullions	22" x 1¼" x 1"

Molding approx. 36' of boards, 1½" or 2"W x ½"T, to be sliced lengthwise

■ Additional Materials

2	Period style metal pulls, oval or flattened "v"-shape
2 pr.	Matching hinges
2	Full mortise locks
2	Strike plates
	Screws
	Wire brads
	Glass for doors

■ Required Tools
5' long bar clamps

I
BUILDING ARTS & CRAFTS FURNITURE

1

First cut, plane, and square all stock. If you don't have wide enough boards for sides and shelves, glue them up. Use biscuits or dowels to join the boards, or spline them. If you plan to use dowels, use a doweling jig to avoid alignment problems. For information about splines and biscuits, see pages 35 and 36.

SIDES AND SHELVES

2

Decide which of the faces of the sides you want to face outward.

3

Before you cut the mortises, make the curve shapes on the tops of the sides and back, and on the bottoms of the sides. A turn-of-the-century home woodworker would have used a coping saw to cut out these shapes.

You can do them that way or you can use a hand-held saber saw, cleaning up the curves with wood rasps, files, and sandpaper. Another approach is make a template of the curve shape, and attach it to the side with screws where the mortise will eventually be cut. Using a sleeve on your router, make a series of light cuts until the shape is cut through. Then clean up the sides of the curve with files or sandpaper.

4

Cut the through mortises for the top and bottom shelves. Cut long blind mortises for the two middle shelves. For more information on cutting mortises, see page 33.

5

Cut the tenons on the ends of the shelves.

For through tenons note that the spacing is critical for the twin tenons to line up properly with the mortises. For more information on cutting tenons, see page 34.

6

Check the fit of the tenons and trim as needed.

7

Bevel the ends of the through tenons.

8

Do your preliminary sanding.

9

Cut the recesses for the doors in the center post. Cut the rabbets that the back will fit into on the top back, bottom back, and

photo 1

sides (photo 1). A router could be used for all, or, the center post and the top and bottom back could be cut on a table saw with a dado blade.

10

Cut blind mortises in the top and bottom shelves for the center post to fit into. The center post should be recessed ³⁄₁₆" from the front of the case.

11

Cut the tenons on the ends of the center post. Cut the dados in the back of the center post where the shelves fit. Mark the hole for the dowel to be drilled (photo 2) and drill holes to dowel the top and bottom back and front pieces.

photo 2

12

Use a doweling jig to drill the holes through the bookcase sides for pinning the top and bottom shelves. It is important to drill these holes straight. The shelf will be in the way once the piece is assembled, so by drilling the holes before assembly, you've eliminated that problem.

13

Sand all the parts made to this point.

14

Dry fit the above parts and then glue up all of them.

15

After the glue is dry, and, using the holes you just drilled as guides, finish drilling through the shelf tenons.

16

Pin the top and bottom shelves with dowels. For more information on doweling joints, see page 36. After the glue dries, sand the dowels flush with the edges of the bookcase sides.

BACK

Early versions of this bookcase used chamfer and spline boards for the back with the characteristic "V" groove between the boards. Later factory versions used a veneered plywood panel to save on labor and materials. Because quartersawn oak plywood is not readily available, and because you want to do quality work, why not opt for the chamfer and spline back? I suggest that you make all the boards the same width for an aesthetically pleasing result, but you may choose any width from approximately 3" up to nearly 8" wide.

17

Measure the cavity to be covered. Determine the width of the boards to be used. (Remember to leave the first and last boards a little over-width to trim later.) Cut the boards to length and width.

18

Cut slots or grooves on the long edges of the boards approximately ½" deep (photo 3). The left side of the left-most board and the right side of the right-most board are not slotted. (The slots should be cut approximately ⅛" from the back side of the board. I used a slot-cutter in a router. These slots could also be cut on a table saw.)

photo 3

19

Cut a slight chamfer 30 to 45 degrees on both edges of the boards on the wider side of each slot. (The chamfer is cut on both edges of the board facing toward its front side.) Be careful that you don't remove too much wood—you don't want to lose any of the slot you just cut. Because you are only cutting on the wider side of the slot, make sure to leave a square edge on the side next to the slot (photo 4). Chamfer all the boards except the left end of the left-most and the right end of the right-most board.

20

Cut a dado on the top and bottom of each board on the inside to fit against the top

photo 4

and bottom of the bookcase assembly (photo 4).

21

Sand the back boards.

22

Cut wood strips for splines for the slots.

23

Glue a strip into one side of each board— do either all the left sides or all the right sides.

24

After the glue dries, test fit the boards against the back of the bookcase, propping them in place, if necessary (photo 5). While they are in place, mark with a pencil on each of these boards the location of each shelf of the bookcase. Make a mark showing both the top and bottom of each shelf. Take down the boards. Use your shelf loca-

photo 5

tion marks on these boards to mark and drill pilot holes for the screws. Countersink the holes from the back.

DOORS

Make sure that the wood that you have selected for the doors is not warped or bowed. It will be difficult to fit the doors if they are not flat.

25

Cut the boards to width.

26

Cut all the boards for the doors about ⅛" longer than your door opening. Subtract ⅜" from the length of the horizontal pieces to allow for the thickness of the hinge supports. Now you may set the mullions aside.

photo 6

27

For the framework of each door: On the verticals (or rails), mark the locations for the ½" mortises for the top and bottom. Do the same for the horizontals (or stiles). Cut the mortises in the frame parts (photo 6).

28

Mark where the locks will go and cut the mortises for them.

photo 7

29

Test fit the locks—they should be recessed slightly (approximately ⅛") (photo 7) .

30

Cut the mortise for the key hole. This mortise may be oversized because it will be covered by the door pull.

31

Cut a ⅜"-wide x ¾"-deep rabbet on the inside of the horizontal and vertical frame parts and on both sides of the mullions (photo 8). The rabbet should line up with the edges of the mortises and leave a ¼"-thick lip on the front of the door pieces .

32

Cut specialized haunched tenons on each end of the horizontal frame parts (photo 9). First cut the 2"-wide x 1/4"-deep rabbet on

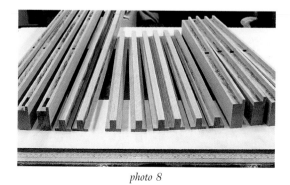

photo 8

photo 9

rabbet on the ends of all horizontal parts, including mullions, and cut a 2½"-wide x ¼"-deep rabbet on both ends of the vertical mullions. Also, make a matching ¼"-deep dado in the center of the horizontal mullions. The width of this dado is sized to the width of the vertical mullion (1¼").

33

Cut a 1⅝"-wide x ¼"-deep rabbet on both ends of the inside of all horizontal parts and cut a 2⅛"-wide x ¼"-deep rabbet on both sides of the vertical mullions. This should produce ½" haunched tenons to fit into the mortises in the vertical and horizontal door frame parts. Trim the sides of the haunched tenons on the horizontal door frame parts.

34

Trim the tenons to match the depth of the mortises.

photo 10

35

Test all joints for fit and trim as necessary.

36

Cut lap joints where the vertical and horizontal mullions intersect. Test the joint for fit (photo 10).

37

Dry assemble the doors, checking for fit. Trim as necessary.

38

Mark and cut the hinge mortises. NOTE: There are specialized jigs for cutting hinge mortises. I used a router freehand to remove most of the wood and cleared out the mortises with a hand chisel.

39

Glue and clamp the doors. After the glue dries, fit the doors to the openings in the cabinet. Use pennies as spacers to create a gap of equal width on the top, bottom, and inside edge of the doors. Trim as necessary using a belt sander or hand plane.

40

The edges of the doors that meet the center post must be beveled 3 to 4 degrees on the inside for the door to close properly. You may hand plane or sand to achieve the bevel.

41

Cut the hinge support strips to size and check for fit between the door and the case sides, trimming and planing as necessary.

42

Holding the doors in place, with pennies as spacers, mark the position of the hinge mortises on the hinge support strips and cut the mortises.

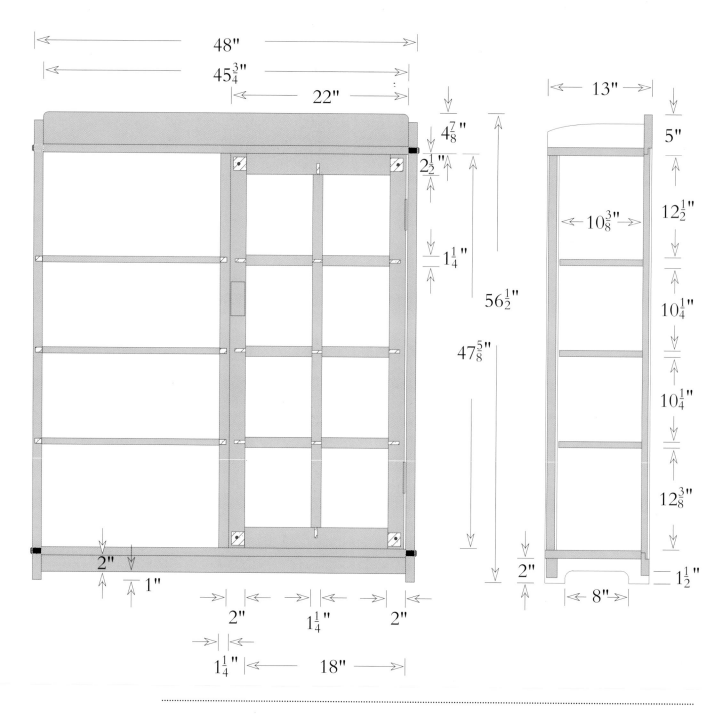

43

Glue the hinge support strips to the inside of the case sides using wire nails as cleats. NOTE: Hinge supports and doors are recessed ³⁄₁₆" from the front edge of the cabinet.

44

After the glue dries, screw the hinges to the case and then to the doors. Re-check for fit, and trim as necessary.

photo 11

photo 12

45

Install the mortise locks. Mark where the lock contacts the center post and cut the mortises in the center post with a hand chisel. Strike plates may not be available for the mortise locks that you buy—they were not available with mine. You can make your own from sheet copper or brass to install on the center post (photo 11).

DOOR MOLDINGS

Each door has 8 individual panes of glass. The glass is held in place by chamfered oak moldings.

46

Plane sufficient stock 1½" or 2" wide x ½" thick to make 36' of stock.

47

Cut a 30 degree chamfer along both edges of the strips.

48

Sand the surfaces.

49

Cut a ¼"- to ⁵⁄₁₆"-wide strip from each edge of board to produce 2 lengths of chamfered molding (photo 12).

50

Miter and fit the molding to the pane openings on the inside of the doors. Number the locations of the molding pieces.

51

Do a final sanding. Your bookcase is now ready to finish. If you plan to ammonia fume your piece, remember to take every scrap of hardware off of it first, or the result will be an unfortunate chemical reaction between the ammonia and the metal. After the finish has dried on the bookcase, remember to sign your work.

GLASS

52

Have the glass cut for the doors. I recommend taking the doors to the person cutting the glass so that the panes may be individually fitted. Instruct the individual to make the glass ⅛" smaller than each opening to allow for expansion.

53

To install: Hold the glass in place with the moldings you previously cut, attaching them with small wire brads. Use a small nail set to recess the brads. Install all of the hardware.

The New Indian Embroidery

Designs Adapted From Native Work

14654
Cushion Design in Stenciling on Crash

14654
Book-Rest Covered With Linen

A Stenciled Folio-Cover

14654
Border in Stenciling and Embroidery

From an article in The Ladies' Home Journal, *1913*

BIBLIOGRAPHY

Arts and Decoration. 1910-1920.

Bennett, Charles Alpheus. *History of Manual and Industrial Education 1870 to 1917.* Peoria: Manual Arts Press, 1937.

Boris, Eileen. *Art and Labor* (Dissertation). Philadelphia: Temple University Press, 1986.

Brown, William H. *The Conversion and Seasoning of Wood.* Fresno, CA: Linden Publishing, 1988.

Coote, Stephen. *William Morris.* New York: Smithmark, 1995.

The Craftsman. 1901-1916.

Darling, Sharon. *Chicago Furniture.* New York: W.W. Norton, 1984.

Eaton, Allen H. *Handicrafts of New England.* New York: Harper Brothers, 1947.

Fidler, Patricia. *Art with a Mission.* Lawrence: Spencer Museum of Art, The University of Kansas, 1991.

Gowans, Alan. *The Comfortable House.* Cambridge, MA: The MIT Press, 1986.

Lynes, Russell. *The Tastemakers.* New York: Harper & Brothers, 1954.

Saylor, Henry H. *Bungalows.* Philadelphia: John C. Winston Co., 1911.

Vallance, Aymer. *William Morris.* London: Studio Editions, 1986.

Wright, Frank Lloyd. *The Natural House.* New York: Horizon Press, 1954.

CONTEMPORARY SOURCES

Stained Glass Design, Lighting
Janine Ody
Cristallo
102 W. Wayne St.
Maumee, OH 43537
(419) 893-5552

Textiles
Dianne Ayres
Arts and Crafts Period Textiles
5427 Telegraph Ave., W2
Oakland, CA 94609
(510) 654-1645

Pottery Tile and Vessels
Pewabic Pottery
10125 E. Jefferson
Detroit, MI 48214
(313) 822-0954

Metalwork
Tony Smith
Buffalo Studios
1925 E. Deere Ave.
Santa Ana, CA 92705
(714) 250-7333

Chris Efker
Craftsman Hardware Co.
P.O. Box 161
Marceline, MO 64658
(816) 376-2481

Etchings
Phillip C. Thompson
30429 White Oak Drive
Bangor, ME 49013
(616) 427-8373

MEASURED DRAWINGS

For information on obtaining enlarged detailed drawings of these book projects write to:

Paul Kemner
P.O. Box 49
Toledo, OH 43697

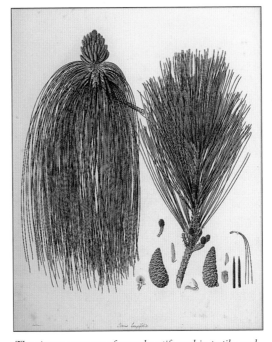

The pinecone was one of several motifs used in textiles and other home decor items during the Arts and Crafts movement.

INDEX